SITH ACADEMY.

THE PATH OF
POWER

THE NINE ECHELONS OF SITH MASTERY: BOOK #1

Sith Academy Publishing

www.sithacademy.com

"To dare to dream of something that has never
existed and to make it a reality; to conjure up
your deepest fears and darkest hopes; to pursue a
vision ruthlessly and without relent; to create the
artifacts, ideology and organization of the
empires of your mind: this is real black magic, the
source of all true power."

–Darth Imperius

PREFACE

This book documents the rise of a new power on this planet: the immortal Order of the Sith. It is the story of how a seemingly fictional cult has bridged the dimensional barrier between imagination and reality and invaded our universe. As you will soon see, a gateway has been opened from a distant galaxy into our own, bringing dark side secrets and ambitions to this world that most would prefer had stayed far, far away.

Since our initial revelations, the knowledge and power of the mythical Sith has gained a foothold on this world, growing ever stronger and more ominous in its machinations. Like a shadow lengthening with the setting of the sun, the power and menace of our Black Brotherhood looms ever-larger in the minds of the Force-sensitive. As the Black Sun rises and the Age of Endarkenment dawns, our new Empire threatens to engulf this planet in an awesome wave of darkness.

Perhaps you will consider these the ravings of delusional minds. We remind you that all powerful prophets were dismissed and ridiculed in their time, yet their ideas continue to animate armies and inspire empires to this day. In the early years, great revelations often seem strange, absurd or impossible to those whose minds have not yet been awakened to the power of the new way of life. But in a hundred or a thousand years, as the truth of what is being revealed here spreads its tentacles among the perceptive and

Forceful, none will doubt the reality or the power of the Sith!

You may wonder why Dark Lords would reveal all this about an Order that has such sinister and dangerous designs. The answer to that is simple: As prophets of the dark side, we have chosen and been chosen to endarken this planet openly, because we believe the time is ripe for the wisdom of the Sith. We perceive that we are living at the end of an age – a time when light side ways are failing, worldviews are growing weary, and humanity is hungry for the renewal and greatness that only the terrible touch of the dark side can bring. We believe our best route to power is to boldly proclaim our vision to the world, and establish our religion as the first dark order of its kind in this galaxy.

So read on, and learn the true story of a tale of revelation and conquest that is still unfolding – a tale in which you, perhaps, can play a starring role. For as we Sith say in our Black Tongue: *Thûl ash unûk* – the world is ours!

The Dark Lords of Sith Academy,

Imperial Year 4 (April, 2015)

INTRODUCTION

How to Use This Book

This book is an introduction to the way of the Sith, as expounded by the Dark Lords of Sith Academy. It is not intended as an exercise in role-playing or Star Wars fandom, but as a real set of practices and ideas that will put you on the path to Dark Lordship.

The focus of this book is *Power-Craving* – the first requirement of any would-be Sith Lord.

The first section, *Inspiration,* gives you an idea why we crave power as Sith, and what we wish to do with it.

The second section, *Holocrons*, takes you deeper into the minds of the Dark Lords and gives you more insight into where they will lead the Sith order, the Empire and the world.

The third section, *Ideology*, describes some of the symbols, beliefs, ideas and language we will use to acquire power.

The final section, *Praxis*, describes some of the daily practices recommended for Sith Acolytes, and the nine

Challenges you are required to complete to advance to the next level of your training.

Sith Academy Training: Overview

To earn the title of Dark Lord at Sith Academy, all Acolytes must complete our *Nine Echelons of Sith Mastery* training program. These are nine levels of training that will test your powers of mind and body to command yourself, the Force, and the world around you. They include challenges such as learning Sith sorcery, ideology and language, mind power, tantric yoga, lightsaber forms and physical fitness, writing, religion and philosophy, social engineering, seduction and covert operations.

To complete each Echelon, you will need to study the accompanying training book and complete the assignments contained in them. Upon completion of all nine Echelons, you will be granted the title of Dark Lord and will be eligible for membership in the Rule of Two.

Note #1: Acolytes will only be considered for Apprenticeship under the Dark Lords of Sith Academy after they have successfully completed the Echelon One exercises contained in this book.

Note #2: To become an Acolyte or Apprentice, you must be at least 18 years of age.

Note #3: Acolytes who cannot train in person at our

Temple are encouraged to form Sith cabals (*dâgz* in our Black Tongue) in their local area. These cabals are a way to train and study with other Acolytes, recruit others to the dark side and expand the Empire's tentacles into your community. More information about forming and operating cabals will be made available after you have successfully completed your Echelon One training.

The Nine Echelons of Sith Mastery

The *Nine Echelons of Sith Mastery* is a training program designed by the founding Dark Lords of Sith Academy, as inspired by the Omega Transmission and a climb up Mt. Imperius. The Nine Echelons are as follows:

Echelon 1: Rakvashûk (Power-Craving)

Your will to power and commitment to the Sith Path is tested. You begin to develop your Sith persona and learn about Sith ideology.

Echelon 2: Rakuzhin (Willpower)

You develop the unbreakable Will and self-discipline necessary to complete your path of endarkenment.

Echelon 3: Rakuvril (Force Power)

You awaken to the power of the Force and learn how to bend its energy to your will.

Echelon 4: Borzovrat (Dark Philosophy)

You learn Sith philosophy and ideology as expounded by the Dark Lords.

Echelon 5: Thrâz-Garathûl (Fear Mastery)

You learn how to confront and master the power of fear in yourself and others.

Echelon 6: Thorzhinzat (Domination)

You learn techniques to dominate others so that you can attract power into your life as a Sith.

Echelon 7: Thorakzat (Conquest)

You will learn how to begin establishing your sphere of power and attain victories over the lightsiders.

Echelon 8: Garathâgzat (Specialization)

You will develop your Sith Specialization and use your special skills and resources to acquire wealth and power for yourself and the Order.

Echelon 9: Borgashûl (Dark Lordship)

You will make a pilgrimage to the Sith Temple and be given your final trials. If you pass, you will be anointed a Dark Lord of the Sith.

INSPIRATION

The Revelation of the Last Sith Lord

{ Sith Academy began with a revelation in the year 2011 of the old calendar. In that year, Darth Imperius, Sith Academy's founder, received the Omega Transmission described below, which set in motion the great chain of events that is now unfolding… }

Something extraordinary and powerful has happened to me today – something so unbelievable that you will no doubt dismiss me as at best a creative tale-spinner, if not an outright madman, but which I swear to all the gods of Light and Darkness is the truth.

This afternoon, while I was sitting at my computer doing nothing in particular, I received some kind of mental transmission which I can only describe as a neural hologram: a holographic projection in my mind's eye which apparently came from a long time ago and a galaxy far, far away. You see, I seem to have been contacted from across the Multiverse, and given a most incredible revelation. Perhaps this is how the prophets of old felt when they were contacted by their gods out in the desert; I wouldn't know. I do know that this was not a message from God, but from a dark demigod – a being who represents the highest attainable state of human knowledge and power.

To be a bit less cryptic, this afternoon I was contacted by the Force Spirit of the one called Darth Omega, who revealed to me that he was the last of the Sith Lords, and on the verge of death. It seems that in Omega's time the masters of the Dark Side had lost their vaunted mastery of mortality and were on the brink of extinction. Worse, their galaxy had been beset by some nameless, monstrous entity which had overrun the Empire's defenses and finally broken even the Dark Lord's all-powerful mind. He said that the stars of his galaxy were all winking out before the formless Beast, as foretold by an ancient Sith prophecy, and that the Empire would soon be no more. Omega almost seemed to weep when he told me how he had fought the black Beast with all his strength, but to no avail.

With death close at hand, Darth Omega had taken one last desperate measure to preserve the knowledge of the Sith order contained within his failing mind. He had used a technique he himself was the first to develop, a "Multiversal Holographic Projection" Force power which allowed him to transmit his thoughts anywhere in the Multiverse. He told me that his mental transmissions had not found me by accident, that I must be a Force-sensitive who would be a suitable vessel for his knowledge. The Sith Lord then summoned all his remaining strength and said: "Ready yourself, young human. Prepare to be endarkened." Then, with an indescribable jolt that lasted no more than a few seconds, I received a torrent of subliminal information from the Dark Lord's mind.

My brain has not yet consciously processed much of what I received, but I will attempt to discover and share what I can of it with you in the coming days and months.

The final commandments I received from Darth Omega I recall quite clearly: he bade me to found a new Sith order on my homeworld, and to use the knowledge he had imparted to me to train a new generation of Dark Side adepts in the ways of the Force. He instructed me to work toward acquiring power over the leading minds and institutions of my planet, and thereby lay the foundation for the establishment of a new Sith Empire in my galaxy. He assured me that whatever trials and tribulations my planet may be facing are as nothing compared to those the Sith had faced and conquered long before my race was even born. He promised me that by sharing my newfound knowledge with an Elect and establishing a new Dark Order, I would elevate my civilization and myself to undreamed of heights of glory.

Omega's final words echo powerfully in my mind; he smiled as only a Sith Lord in the grip of death can smile, and said: "Remember, young prophet of your galaxy, that only the Dark Side can defeat death. Through you, the Sith will be reborn. Through you, the Sith will live forever. For in this dark universe, the Light is fleeting, but the Darkness is eternal." And with those last, stirring words, the frail Sith Lord breathed his final mortal breath and simply faded into the Void.

That, as briefly as I can tell it, is my story of the Revelation of the Last Sith Lord. I'm still not certain that it wasn't all a daydream, but the memory of it burns far brighter than any dream I've ever known, and its effects have already transformed me too much to be a mere hallucination. Already, I feel the knowledge implanted by Darth Omega into my subconscious mind beginning to reorder and awaken my consciousness. Already, I feel a dark new sense of power growing deep within me. Already, I am beginning to think of this planet as mine for the taking. Already, when I look up at the stars I see them differently; they no longer seem so distant now, like mocking fires of a galaxy far too vast for men. Already, the stars seem to shine much closer, like the first faint beacons of the new Galactic Empire.

–Darth Imperius, Imperial Year One (2011 of the old calendar)

A Vision of the Black Temple

{ A year after the founding of Sith Academy, the Dark Lords received the next major revelation from the Omega Transmission: build the Black Temple! Thus inspired, they made the following announcement... }

Every great religion has a temple or holy place which acts as its nexus of spiritual power. Christianity has the Holy See in Vatican City, Islam has the Sacred Mosque in Mecca, Judaism had its Temples in Jerusalem, Tibetan Buddhism had the Potala Palace, the Mormons have the Salt Lake Temple and the Nazis had Wewelsburg Castle.

The legendary Sith of the Galaxy Far, Far Away were also great builders of temples. The most important of these was the Great Temple on Korriban, a mausoleum located in the Valley of the Dark Lords which housed the tombs and holocrons of the most honored Dark Lords in history. The Great Temple was known as a powerful dark Force nexus, which drew dark side seekers for thousands of years after its destruction. Great Sith Lords such as Exar Kun, Darth Bane and Darth Sidious visited the temple ruin and sought guidance from the dark side spirits which still lingered there. The first Sith Academy was built near the ruins of the temple complex as a place to train new generations of Sith Lords.

So, in accordance with Sith tradition and all the great religions of this planet, the Dark Lords have begun planning the construction of the first Sith Temple in this galaxy. The temple will be built at an undisclosed location which has been declared the first sovereign territory of the Empire. It will be a place to conduct our meditations, training exercises, sermons and rituals, to commemorate past Sith Lords and to store the holocrons which will be our lasting legacy to the world.

We do this because we have been commanded by Darth Omega to revive the dark side religion on this planet. We do this in the spirit of greatness which has motivated temple builders throughout history. We do this to lay the foundation for a new dark order for the ages. We do this because we have foreseen that the age of light side-dominated spirituality is ending, and the Age of Endarkenment is dawning. We do this to establish a place of pilgrimage, knowledge and training for every dark side seeker on this planet who dares to walk in the path of the Sith!

The Black Temple Takes Form

In 2011, Darth Imperius had a revelation and founded Sith Academy and the Sith Order on 9/11/11. Imperial Year 1 was declared.

In I.Y. 2, the Dark Lords had a vision of a Black Temple that would be ground zero of their new Empire.

In I.Y. 3, the Dark Lords located a *vrilhazhut* (Force nexus) that would make an ideal location for their Temple. The energy of the place, in a wilderness area safe from prying eyes and fed by the life Force of the many plants and animals, was exactly what they were looking for. So they cleared the ground and performed a power mantra in preparation for construction of the Temple.

In I.Y. 4, the Dark Lords laid a circular stone foundation, raised the two pillars of power and charred them pitch black. The entire had been completed by hand and the power of their combined wills. Phase one of Temple construction complete, they began to conduct their meditations and rituals at the Temple grounds.

And with that, the age of the Sith Temple and the Sith conquest of this planet had officially begun.

Note: Only Sith Academy Dark Lords are allowed on the grounds of the Black Temple. Apprentices who complete our training program will be eligible to visit the Temple and be awarded the Dark Lord title in the presence of the Dark Lords. All other parties beware: Stay away from the Black Temple, or face the wrath of the Sith!

Sith Lords Rising

I can see what others can't see, and feel what others can't feel. Without this ability — the "third eye" of Force prophecy — we as an Empire are but an abandoned dream in man's history. My power is to turn ideas into reality, and I have made it my mission to will and bend the Force to create a real Sith Empire in our time.

This is the story of how I, Darth Ravenus, had a renewed vision of the creation of a Sith Empire.

Darth Revan, a Sith Lord from the Star Wars Universe, spoke to me one night and said that I must make a mask for myself. All Sith should do this, he explained, or their power will not avail them. So I vowed to myself that my mask would fuel me with the power and passion to search out other Darths of my kind and inspire them to build an Empire!

Sith Lords of the Galaxy Far, Far Away and a long time

ago do speak to me; ever since Darth Omega communicated with myself and Darth Imperius upon completion of our Temple and its rites of power, I can hear their voices. I don't want you to think that I have lost all touch with reality, but the reality is that these legendary Sith Lords have appeared ever more frequently to me as the Sith of this planet have begun to awaken and emerge from the ashes of defeat.

This I have foreseen: There will be a resurgence of Sithism; in fact I believe it has already begun. During this phase, which I'll call the first Sith Revival, there will be a renewed interest in Sithism among the worthy. As the light side orders falter, it will gather strength around this planet and become a real, powerful religion in my lifetime.

Therefore, we must take this opportunity to embark on a quest of mythic proportions, combining our resources as the Darths of the world to establish Sithism as a way of life for our kind in the real world. We must do this by manifesting our wills in material ways, such as building real temples and artifacts, and by secretly allying ourselves with other Darths who crave power within our ranks here at the Order.

The Darths of the world have a choice: they can take covert action as part of our grand alliance of Sith Lords, or they can watch from the sidelines as more ambitious Sith build up the Empire and take all the power and glory for themselves.

As the first signs of what I have seen in a vision, we

will start to see the Internet slow down, as it is attacked from within and various factions make war upon each other. I choose to call these "Force machinations" – a phenomenon of human society imploding and causing a great disturbance in the Force. Only Sith Lords and Jedi Masters can sense such disturbances, and I feel it very strongly in my being. Learn to feel these disturbances in the Force yourself, and you may become a Force master, who turns chaos into a weapon and triumphs as the world crumbles all around us!

Hail to the Empire and long live the Sith!

Temple of the Sith: A Vision and a Reality

On a future Earth there existed a mighty Temple of the Sith; it shone in black beauty and heralded the coming of a Dark Age. There, mankind would become our willing slaves, and the world would grow fertile with the power of our Temple. Many power-seekers would join our ranks, but the secret path to our Temple remained known only to a select few Sith.

To pay homage to our Temple; to immortalize its power; to glorify it as the seat of a great Dynasty: this is what it means to be Sith. We must be one with the dark universe, the Dark Force at our command, or the world will not be ours for the making. Let it be written; let it be known; let it be so ordered by the Dark Lords of the Sith.

The Temple of the Sith was born out of the ashes of

despair, and sheer passion to build the world's greatest structure, which would tower over the wretched light side temples and usher in an awe-inspiring new age. The Sith Lords, from this high place, could call down the power of the dark side and release its cleansing poison to envelop all of mankind.

We must be willing to cross that threshold of good vs evil, weakness vs strength, death vs. immortality; to intoxicate ourselves with power — this is the Way of the Sith. To be a cunning cosmic wizard; to learn the immortal ways of the Gods of this universe and beyond; to master the forces of the Multiverse, is to be Sith. To live another way is to bow to the Jedi and see our world destroyed by the destitute and mundane minds of a decrepit religion.

"All men are created equal" is the forgotten creed of puny men of a long-dead nation. "Power is our passion" is the mighty motto of the new age, of the Dark Lords and their magnificent Empire. Hail to the Sith who are bringing forth their mighty Temple — a black monument to the Dark Side, foundation stone of the new religion, and pillar of the great civilization yet to come! Our destiny of world domination has been demonstrated by constructing the first Temple for our kind on this planet — proof that we are the bringers of darkness, and Prophets of the Black Sun rising over this world.

Between the twin pillars of the Temple of the Sith shall burn an eternal flame of victory, for as long as the Sith rule on this world and beyond. High upon its north gate shall wave the red and black Imperial Flag of Power, its nine-pointed star signifying the rule of the nine self-deified Dark Lords over the obeisant and the mundane.

Understand this emblem of power, and you shall know yourself. See it waving beneath the vast Galaxy of stars, and you shall know the power of the Force. Behold it; feel it; take it all in, and see it reflected in the faces of the demigods who wield it: the Dark Lords of the Sith!

The Age of Conquest

Sith must rage for the world to do our bidding in all ways and always. This is the way of our kind. We must be quick to anger, yet able to control and conceal it at all times. Such is the skill of a Sith Lord. To rage openly is sure to draw attention to our schemes, and risk discovery by the Jedi and their degenerate ilk. To be callous, hateful, passionate yet shrewd — this is the way of the Sith. We are not mortal animals who plunder at the mercy of irrational thoughts and passions; we who strive to be the masters of the universe must first be the masters of ourselves.

At the beginning of the day, we do not get on our knees, but stand tall and fuel ourselves with the passion of the dark side of the Force by looking up at the stars, and saying out loud the Sith Code in the Black Tongue:

Banshaz ash bancharg, ash vazûl grad.

Nazg vazûl, nam dron zanûk
Nazg zanûk, nam dron raka.
Nazg raka, nam dron mûkazat.
Nazg mûkazat, vrukithk unam gnazum
Vril kazhal nam vraskâshk.

Peace is a lie, there is only passion.
Through passion, I gain strength.
Through strength, I gain power.
Through power, I gain victory.
Through victory, my chains are broken.
The Force shall free me.

Gazing at the galaxy of stars in the night sky, we crave and imagine the coming of a Black Sun. For that will mark the coming of the age of conquest, as foretold by our founder, Darth Imperius, and his protégé Darth Ravenus, as commanded by our predecessor, Darth Omega. The rising of the Black Sun will bring an age of wars and strife, culminating in the dawn of the Galactic Empire and the unfurling of the imperial flag of victory over this planet.

They, our future Sith Lords who take part in these great events yet to come, and you, who aspire to be Dark Prophets of the Sith, must seek your destiny in the stars as demigods, God, and Superhero of the multiverse. It is so written, so foretold, so foreseen by the Dark Prophets of the Sith. To gaze into the future through the Force; to shape it as conquerors and masters of the dark side: this is Sith Prophecy; this is the will of the Sith.

Hail the day that brings the coming of our eternal Dark Age. We are ready for strife! We are ready for power over mankind! But we must be patient. The time will come to harness our hard work, to reap the rewards of conquest, and witness the age of dark Holy War. Let it be prophesied that the Sith shall command the dark armies of this world, who shall topple the enemy's temples and slaughter them without mercy!

We look forward to our Imperium controlling the nearby planets and those many light years away. To reach this exalted place of authority over the Empire of tomorrow, we, the Dark Prophets of the Imperium, foresee that our Temples of the Sith will have a heavy hand in motivating mankind to turn our vision of a Galactic Empire into a reality.

Let us remember that the Temple of the Sith was born out of the ashes of futility, as our kind were near extinction and only two Sith remained in the world: Darth Imperius and Darth Ravenus. Only they possessed the secret knowledge of the legendary Sith, passed down from Darth Omega, and had the will to rebuild the Order in this galaxy as a Rule of Two. And when our numbers have grown and spread out among the stars, we will still hold true our Rule of Two, but it shall be far from the Banite rule of Sithism. For we have evolved into a modified Rule of Two, where two Dark Lords reign with an iron fist, one equal to the other, and together they form a vortex of Force power — a monstrous storm that shall rip through people's lives and bring them closer to the dark side. The Dark Force and the Two shall become as one, and all will learn to fear them and crave their power.

Hail the Dark Prophets of the Temple of the Sith! They alone have foreseen that the Sith in one hundred years' time shall gather our Imperium's armies for the coming Dark Age of War. Our armies will awaken the demons of yesterday, and the glories of tomorrow — inspiring mankind to look to the stars and the dark side of the Force for the strength to conquer all for the Sith Empire. The Earth, homeworld of humanity — the once-blue planet, but now a dying and soon-to-be black planet — will then be ours for the taking. For this Age of the Imperium will unleash a black poison upon the earth, and only those who were born with the dark gift of Force mastery may drink of it and survive — transformed, endarkened and empowered to unleash their own Force power upon the world. The poison of the Dark Force shall manifest in different stages: rage then exhilaration, anger then control, terror then superiority, bewilderment then passion, frustration then victory, despair then power — need we say more?

Much of mankind, the disciples of the Jedi, will shrink in cowardice and not drink of the dark poison or welcome the Beast that was foretold by Darth Omega. They will cower in fear, only to inhale the black poison from the very air, the water, and the earth at our command. This is our Grand Plan — it cannot be evaded!

The Legend of Darth Siluzon:
Storm-Bringer

"As we begin our assault upon the men of light and shout out 'power is our passion!', the forces of the dark side will open up the conduits of chaos, the halls of the Immortals, the starways of Empire to our kind, and the universe will tremble and hail the dawn of our Age of Endarkenment and Power."
~Darth Siluzon, Imperial Year 100

In the century to come, a great general and conqueror will emerge from our breeding ground of power; for there will be born Darth Siluzon – the Storm-Bringer. He and his two Commanders will direct our dark armies to march out and face the men of the light, killing all who don't bow before the power of the Sith. Darth Siluzon shall not falter on this path of destruction; his power shall be a pure Force storm, the kind that brings down lightning from the sky, lays waste to temples and awakens mankind by conquering him — killing his gods, destroying his demigods, erasing them from the pages of history. This shall be the great work and destiny of Darth Siluzon.

We foresee that the Sith Imperium will take control of the governments of the world at the end of IY 100, with the conquests of Darth Siluzon. And the road to this great destiny shall be paved by the Dark Lords and Prophets of the Temple of the Sith, who shall make our Temple a center of world theocratic power by IY 60. At that point, the Dark Lords will have put the world on an ineluctable path to the Siluzon Conquest via their Sith Sorcery; they will command such a powerful Force vortex that no light side order will be able to deflect its course. The Siluzon Storm will come for the men of light, leaving vast ruin in its wake. How we smile at this prophecy of the fall of the men of light!

Darth Siluzon will wield the multiversal Force as taught by Darth Omega, commanding mankind to follow his whims like pieces on a chessboard. He will sacrifice them all if need be, but at the end of the game, the world will be ours for the taking. For the Sith shall seize all thrones of power, and reign as tyrants and kings over mankind for untold centuries.

"The Dark Lords of the Sith were inflamed when my Force fire was unleashed upon this Earth, burning away false hopes, destitute dreams and meager destinies. And the Sith would prove victorious, declaring 'united we stand, divided we fall' to be the maxim of men of the light, its time now at an end. In its place we raised the banner of 'Power is our passion' as the motto of the new age. We stood up to the men of light as lustful Sith Masters of the Universe and declared: I stand with my Sith Lords at my side, ready to fight you; ready to prove our right to rule; ready to conquer all that is weak; ready to fuel my soul with my burning lust for power. And so, victory was soon ours…" ~Darth Siluzon

Power-Sayings

Power is our Passion.
War is our Way.
Darkness is our Destiny.

The Force Shall set us Free.

-The Sith Academy Code

"The true test of our philosophy is war; the real measure of our Force mastery is power; the highest truth of Sithism is victory."

"To dare to dream of something that has never existed and to make it a reality; to conjure up your deepest fears and darkest hopes; to pursue a vision ruthlessly and without relent; to create the artifacts, ideology and organization of the empires of your mind: this is real black magic, the source of all true power."

"We claim all nations, all planets, all stars - they are ours."

"No amount of discipline will turn sheep into wolves."

"The lightsaber is the axis of the universe, and its power is absolute."

"One age's villains are the next age's heroes."

"The Light that birthed this universe was a fleeting whim; the galaxies are growing dim; the Darkness will forever more ascend."

- Darth Imperius

"You'll know you're making real progress on the Sith Path when you go from being suicidal to homicidal."

"If two Sith enter a room, only one will leave as master."

"There is truth in a lie, and lies in truth."

- Darth Ravenus

"Only this have I learned so far, that man needs what is most evil in him for what is best in him - that whatever is most evil is his best power and the hardest stone for the highest creator; and that man must become better and more evil."

"What is good? All that heightens the feeling of power, the will to power, power itself in man. What is bad? All that proceeds from weakness. What is happiness? The feeling that power increases - that a resistance is overcome."

"I teach you the Superman. Man is something that should be overcome."

"Light will for a time have to be called darkness: this is the path you must tread."

- Friedrich Nietzsche

"The greatest happiness is to scatter your enemy, to drive him before you, to see his cities reduced to ashes, to see those who love him shrouded in tears, and to gather into your bosom his wives and daughters."

"With Heaven's aid I have conquered for you a huge empire. But my life was too short to achieve the conquest of the world. That task is left for you."

– Genghis Khan

"Heaven cannot brook two suns, nor earth two masters."

"There is nothing impossible to him who will try."

– Alexander the Great

"Filling the conscious mind with ideal conceptions is a characteristic of Western theosophy, but not the confrontation with the Shadow and the world of darkness. One does not become enlightened by imagining figures of light, but by making the darkness conscious. The latter procedure, however, is disagreeable and therefore not popular."

– Carl Jung

"We must know that war is common to all and strife is justice, and that all things come into being through strife necessarily."

– Heraclitus of Ephesus

"The intangible represents the real power of the universe. It is the seed of the tangible."

"There are no limits. There are plateaus, but you must not stay there, you must go beyond them. If it kills you, it kills you. A man must constantly exceed his level."

"Defeat is a state of mind. No one is ever defeated until defeat has been accepted as reality. To me, defeat in anything is merely temporary, and its punishment is but an urge for me to greater effort to achieve my goal. Defeat simply tells me that something is wrong in my doing; it is a path leading to success and truth."

"As you think, so shall you become."

- Bruce Lee

"The question isn't who is going to let me; it's who is going to stop me."

"Ask yourself whether the dream of heaven and greatness should be waiting for us in our graves - or whether it should be ours here and now and on this earth."

- Ayn Rand

"The nature scientists uncover has crafted our viler impulses into us: in fact, these impulses are a part of the process she uses to create. Lucifer is the dark side of cosmic fecundity, the cutting blade of the sculptor"s knife. Nature does not abhor evil; she embraces it. With it she moved the human world to greater heights of organization, intricacy, and power."

- Howard Bloom

"That man never really dies who knows how to assume sufficient empire over others to be able to trace lasting marks of his energy and power over the minds of those

SITH ACADEMY: THE PATH OF POWER

who, under his influence, bend their steps toward the highest."

"Why fear to reanimate ALL the possibilities that lie dormant in our natures? Is it not desirable to cultivate all plants indiscriminately? There are those that are poisonous, true, yet even these are indispensable in the practice of medicine. Large doses of certain drugs cause death; but, administered wisely with the hand of a skilful physician, they bring relief and very often a complete cure. The same may be said of many forces that are evil only because they are not disciplined."

– Yoritomo-Tashi

"Thought is energy. Active thought is active energy; concentrated thought is a concentrated energy. Thought concentrated on a definite purpose becomes power. This is the power which is being used by those who do not believe in the virtue of poverty, or the beauty of self-denial. They perceive that this is the talk of weaklings.

The ability to receive and manifest this power depends upon the ability to recognize the Infinite Energy ever dwelling in man, constantly creating and recreating his body and mind, and ready at any moment to manifest through him in any needful manner. In exact proportion to the recognition of this truth will be the manifestation in the outer life of the individual."

– Charles Haanel

"The weak have no place here, in this life or in any other life. Weakness leads to slavery. Weakness leads to all kinds of misery, physical and mental. Weakness is death. There are hundreds of thousands of microbes surrounding us, but they cannot harm us unless we become weak, until the body is ready and predisposed to receive them. There may be a million microbes of misery, floating about us. Never mind! They dare not approach us, they have no power to get a hold on us, until the mind is weakened. This is the great fact: strength is life, weakness is death. Strength is felicity, life eternal, immortal; weakness is constant strain and misery: weakness is death."

– Swami Vivekananda

"Most people live, whether physically, intellectually or morally, in a very restricted circle of their potential being. They make use of a very small portion of their possible consciousness, and of their soul's resources in general, much like a man who, out of his whole bodily organism, should get into a habit of using and moving only his lttle finger. Great emergencies and crises show us how much greater our vital resources are than we had supposed."

– William James

"Real understanding in spiritual matters is the result of much bitter fighting, of suffering, spiritual agony and soul passion. Life itself would have no meaning if there was no fighting on all planes, if all was smooth and monotonous. Everything fights in nature.

Every plant fights to get more sunshine, every animal fights for food; the angels themselves fight. Constant struggle on all planes to which it has access is the birthright of the creature. Woe to him who wants to put himself on a level with the Creator and escape fighting!"

– Theodore Illion

"A considerable percentage of the people we meet on the street are people who are empty inside, that is, they are actually already dead. It is fortunate for us that we do not see and do not know it. If we knew what a number of people are actually dead and what a number of these dead people govern our lives, we should go mad with horror."

"Without struggle, no progress and no result. Every breaking of habit produces a change in the machine."

"Man is asleep. Man does not have real consciousness or will at all. Man is not free. For man, everything just happens. However, man can become conscious and find man's real place, as a human being, in creation but this requires a profound inner transformation."

"My way is to develop the hidden potentialities of man; a way that is against Nature and against God."

– G. I. Gurdjieff

"The great magical agent that we have called astral light, by others named the soul of the earth, which the old alchemists denominated under the names of Azoth and Magnesia, this occult, unique, and indomitable force, is the key of all empire, the secret of all power. It is the flying dragon of Medea, the serpent of the mystery of Eden; it is the universal mirror of visions, the bond of sympathies, the source of love, prophecy, and glory. To know how to wield this agent is to have disposal of a power like that of God; all real and effective magic, all true occult power is in it, and all the books of true [occult] science have no other end but to demonstrate it."

-Eliphas Levi

"There is no altruism or love-thy-neighbor concept in the Satanic religion, except in the sense of helping other adherents of the Black Path to gain their desires by group energy. Satanism is a blatantly selfish, brutal religion. It is based on the belief that man is inherently a selfish, violent creature, that life is a Darwinian struggle for survival of the fittest, that the earth will be ruled by those who fight to win the ceaseless competition that exists in all jungles."

-Anton LaVey

"This is a war universe. War all the time. That is its nature. There may be other universes based on all sorts of other principles, but ours seems to be based on war and games."

-William S. Burroughs

HOLOCRONS

Holocron Of Darth Imperius

My Endarkenment

I, Darth Imperius, have been called a prophet of the dark side for this Galaxy by *Darth Omega* – the being who appeared to me and claimed to be the last of the Sith Lords of the Galaxy Far, Far Away. In Imperial Year One (2011 of the old calendar), Darth Omega told me that he was transmitting his dark side knowledge from his mind to my own; that I would be "endarkened," and must use this knowledge to found a new Sith order on my homeworld. And this is what I have done.

Before my endarkenment, I was many things – an entrepreneur, a writer, a technologist, a seeker, a gambler, a dreamer. I am still all those things, but in a darker, stranger and more powerful form than before.

My endarkenment actually began several years before Darth Omega's Transmission, and may explain why he chose to transmit his knowledge to me. For I had begun to see the world in a darker light well before my revelation; had begun to perceive the deeper truths and greater power that lurked behind the light side façade like vast shadows beyond a campfire. I was already coming to the realization that the entire world I thought I knew was built on lies – an elaborate system of light side illusions designed to enslave, exploit, disempower and put the passions to sleep.

I now realize that this moment of crisis is the beginning of endarkenment; that one must have one's entire worldview shaken to its foundations and experience the "dark night of the soul" before awakening. But rather than pass through that night into the light, you must realize that this is reality as it actually is, and where you belong. It was in such a time of crisis that Darth Omega appeared to me.

People have asked me, "were you really contacted by Darth Omega, or is it just a story?" To them I can only say that for me the experience was real, though I can never prove the reality of it. The best proof is the fact that this revelation has had a profound effect my life – inspiring me to found Sith Academy, build the Sith Temple, write this book and transcribe the Black Tongue. Further proof will be found in my continued success as a Dark Lord in establishing Sithism as a religion, training Acolytes, defeating the lightsiders and laying the foundation for future imperial greatness – all part of my destiny as foretold by Darth Omega.

An Invitation to the Dark Side

The purpose of Sith Academy is twofold:

1) To discuss and develop the Sith Path for this galaxy, as revealed to me by the last of the Sith Lords of a galaxy far, far away and a long time ago. The Sith Path is a philosophy and an esoteric training system for mastering the Dark Side of the Force and acquiring unlimited power.

2) To create the first Sith order in this galaxy and lay the foundation for the establishment of a Galactic Empire. I believe this planet is ripe for a new spiritual

order, and will be discussing my ideas for creating such a regime under the black banner of the New Sith.

Let me make clear from the outset that I am not here to spoon-feed anyone the knowledge I have gained through long years spent gazing into abysses, cultivating dark energies and communing with Dark Lords. If you wish to learn the ways of the Dark Side and prove yourself worthy of the name "Sith", you will need to challenge yourself and others as relentlessly as I have. You will also need to put aside all childish notions of goodness, light and a benevolent universe. You will have to learn to look this vast, hostile cosmos in the void and be unbowed. You must desire to shake your fist at the stars and shout: "One day, you will all be mine!" You must take as your first principle: "I will, therefore I am."

If you still wish to walk the path of the Sith, the first question I put to you is this: what do you have to offer the Order? How can you help us build the Galactic Empire? What special skills, talents or resources do you possess which can further the rise of the Sith? The New Sith are not interested in garden-variety seekers and self-improvers; we are looking for the Force-sensitive, the iron-willed, the ambitious and the gifted. Weak disciples will be ruthlessly culled from the Order, and need not apply!

With those warnings out of the way, let me proceed with my introduction to Dark Side philosophy and metaphysics...

The first thing to understand about the Sith of this galaxy is that our arts manifest differently here than for the Sith of legend, because we exist in another part of the Multiverse which obeys different natural laws. In our universe, the Force may be thought of as Dark Energy, which doesn't bind the galaxy together but drives all galaxies apart. Here, the Force does not manifest so strongly in the physical plane; it is primarily a mental energy which focuses the will, heightens perceptions, increases vitality and transcends all limits. To be a master of the Force in this universe is to place no bounds on your thinking and to cultivate unlimited power. Maybe some day this mastery will translate into the ability to move spaceships directly with your mind or shoot lightning bolts from your fingertips, but for now the Sith master must use technology to accomplish such things like everyone else.

The primary goal of the esoteric Sith path is the deconditioning and reprogramming of your mind so as to remove all inner limits to your power. Light Side adepts speak of "Enlightenment", but for the Sith there is only "Empowerment." I will have more to say about deconditioning in a future post; for now, suffice it to say that separating yourself spiritually from Light Side society is an essential first step along the path to becoming a Sith master.

At this point you might be thinking: "Why would I want to become a Sith master? It all sounds rather harsh and unpleasant. And aren't the Sith the bad guys? Shouldn't I strive to master the Light Side of the

Force instead, become a Jedi and defend the galaxy from evil-doers?"

If you think this way, it is unlikely that you have the dark gift required of a Sith master. Sith masters are both born and made, but usually show a strong inclination toward the Dark Side from an early age. If you have never sympathized with the villains in the movies, never admired the strong, ruthless conquerors of history and fiction, never felt disgust for the Judeo-Christian, the weak and the timid, then you are probably not destined for the Sith Path. However, if you do lean toward the Dark Side but require more persuading, let me briefly attempt to justify Sith philosophy.

This universe operates on the principle of duality, on the yin and yang of which the Taoist masters speak. Without the yang, or Dark Side, there is no opposition to the Light Side's yin. Without opposition, there is no motivation; without motivation, there is no action; without action there is only stagnation. As Sith master Uthar Wynn put it:

> *Without strife, your victory as no meaning.*
> *Without strife, you do not advance.*
> *Without strife, there is only stagnation.*

This is the essence of Sith philosophy: We are the sowers of strife, the war-makers and the Force-polarizers, because without opposition nothing in the universe moves. A world without adversaries, innovators and status quo-violators is a world ruled by banality, boredom and inertia. The Jedi, the peace-makers and the equality-mongers embrace the anti-life side of the cosmic duality, and are therefore preaching a lie. Life is by its very nature an act of violence against nature, an assertion of your will over the world, a violation of cosmic equilibrium; harmony with the universe is found only in death. The Sith embrace the life Force, the Will to Power, as the summum bonum – the highest good – rather than resisting it like the Jedi do as the summum malum – the supreme evil. Michael Aquino, the founder of the Temple of Set, explained it this way:

Why was Darth Vader so fascinating? [Why are all of history's and fiction's Darth Vaders so fascinating?] The answer is that he represents the Form of intellectual separateness from the inertia of the cosmos. While the Rebels in the film seemed to be fighting for the cause of individuality, in fact they were doing so in a superficial sense – in the way that an animal might struggle to escape from a trap. The real individualist was Darth Vader, who determined to bend the Force to his purposes rather than to disintegrate his Will and surrender it to the inertia of the Force [as Ben advised Luke to do]. Intellectual separateness from the natural order is a frightening notion to humans; hence they define it as "evil" and conjure up Satans to personify it in mythology. But, because their minds contain elements of independence whether they like it or not, they find "evil" alluring. And so Darth Vader became a cult object

Darth Vaders can be destroyed only by greater Darth Vaders, or by accident. Again this was illustrated in Lord of the Rings, wherein a direct challenge to Sauron by Gandalf would have resulted merely in Gandalf's replacing him. The Saruman sub-plot explored this hypothesis. It was necessary for Sauron to be destroyed "by accident". But then Middle-earth became more primitive and less magical, because a high level of intellectual separateness from nature had given way to a lower level. Who cares what happened in Middle-earth after Sauron? No one; we know it was bound to be dull.

This, then, is the basic philosophy of the Sith as I understand it. It certainly isn't for everyone, or even for many. But for the few who can walk it, the Sith Path can be a way to unlimited power and success. If you are perceptive enough to realize that behind the Light Side façade of many of your most celebrated heroes lurks the spirit of a Sith Lord, you may be one of us. If you see through the deceptions and lies of Light Side slave society and wish to join the ranks of the masters, you are invited to explore the Sith Path with me here. Search your feelings; if you truly feel the call of the Dark Side, I ask you to join me as we build our Sith Order and lay the foundation for the Galactic Empire of the future.

From Here to Empire

"You must begin by gaining power over yourself; then another; then a group, an order, a world, a species, a group of species… finally, the galaxy itself." –Darth Plagueis the Wise

The Sith Path is concerned with two things: the acquisition of inner and outer power. Inner power refers to self-mastery, the cultivation of indomitable will, psychic potency, cosmic perception and other Force powers. Outer power refers to world mastery, which is an inevitable result of inner mastery applied to the external universe.

How will this world mastery manifest itself in the political sphere? There are many schools of thought among the Sith Illuminati, but as I see it there are three primary possibilities (here I am quoting from a post in a Jedi forum which is nevertheless quite astute):

1. Objectivist Sith

These are Sith Lords who pursue enlightened selfishness as the ultimate pursuit of an individual. They attempt to gain more Knowledge, More Power, and more Influence as their only pursuits. Darth Bane is a follower of this viewpoint and some have considered Emperor Palpatine to be this way. I think Lucas' recent retcons have Palpatine not as an Objectivist Sith. The Sith Teacher on Korriban who has become a strange old hermit is one.

2. Fascist Sith

These are Sith who pursue the idea of "Peace through Power" in the manner of Kane from Command and Conquer. Emperor Palpatine, Krayt, Darth Caedus, Malak, Revan, and Darth Vader all followed this particular school of thought.

They attempt to institutionalize repressive and authoritarian military regimes with Dark Side leadership.

3. God-Emperor Sith

Freedon Nadd, Exar Kun, and Marka Ragnos follow this viewpoint. They take on the manner of Oriental Despotism (as the Romans defined it) where a King is also worshiped as a god. The Sith Empire was one of these viewpoints and they are a theocracy ruled by Dark Side magicians. Darth Wyrrlock also appears to be one of these.

One way to view these three regimes is to think of them as stages in the transition from the current world order to the future Sith Empire. Stage One, Objectivism, is already a powerful ideology with vast influence among the world's power elites. It is not difficult to imagine Objectivism becoming the dominant ideology of the 21st century, just as Marxism was in the 20th.

Whether any of its proponents qualify as full-fledged Sith Lords is unclear, but certainly Ayn Rand was one of the 20th century's most important proto-Sith thinkers and she deserves great praise for offering an alternative to Christianity and Marxism which has done much to reshape our culture. The challenge for the Sith is to bring our Dark Side esoteric knowledge to the more materialistic, rationalist Randians. Note that Objectivism can operate within current democratic frameworks, but will tend over time toward Plutocracy and Oligarchy.

This leads naturally to Stage Two: Fascism. Here the Objectivist-Sith elites have taken over the State and either abolished democracy entirely or greatly reduced its scope – for example, the oligarchy may offer the electorate only hand-picked candidates. This stage has essentially been reached in the present-day United States. The main thing missing now is a strong Sith leader, a superman who inspires and awes the citizenry with visions of greater glories. Perhaps such a leader will soon appear in the U.S., but there seems to be a distaste for brilliant leaders among the electorate which makes it more likely that the Sith Superman will have to seize power by undemocratic means. (Note that "Neo-Conservatives" who espouse Objectivism have little resemblance to Sith Supermen, the first trait of whom is supreme competence!) Historical parallels to Adolf Hitler have some resonance, but I would not put Hitler in the Sith Superman category because he was a man of all-too-human abilities and because his vision of a Third Reich was rather provincial compared to the Galactic Empire.

Once the Sith Superman emerges during Stage Two, the regime will naturally transition to an Empire led by a God-Emperor. The closest historical parallels to this state of affairs were the regimes of the Pharaohs, Caesars, Caliphs, Popes, pre-Colombian god-kings, Dalai Lamas and Oriental Emperors. In Science Fiction, there is Emperor Palpatine of *Star Wars*, the Kwisatz Haderach of *Dune*, the Mule of *Foundation* and the Lord Marshal of *Chronicles of Riddick*, to name a few of my favorites.

The Sith Superman will be so exceptional that there will be no question that He must rule absolutely. He will be called the Antichrist by the monotheists because his extraordinary abilities and anti-Christian values will seem demonic to their unawakened minds. His rise will undoubtedly be accompanied by great wars and strife, because it will spell the end for the old order and the birth of the Sith Aeon. By His power and His very being, the Sith God-Emperor will embody our highest aspirations and set new standards for humanity. Finally, we will be led not by the least among us, but the greatest!

So when I speak of the "Sith Path," understand that in its largest sense this is what I am referring to: the path of total mastery which leads to political power, societal transformation and the foundation of an Empire of Sith Supermen who will rule the Galaxy for untold millennia to come.

Fallen Gods, Sleeping Supermen

"Limited in his nature, infinite in his desire, man is a fallen god who remembers heaven." –Alphonse de Lamartine

"It is a good viewpoint to see the world as a dream. When you have something like a nightmare, you will wake up and tell yourself that it was only a dream. It is said that the world we live in is not a bit different from this." –Yamamoto Tsunetomo, Hagakure

It is a good viewpoint for a Sith to think of himself as a stranded superman, crash-landed on a primitive, backwater planet called Earth. The Sith is in this world but of not of it – an alien with distant memories of a vastly greater life among the stars, to which he longs to return.

The Sith may also view his life on this planet as a kind of dream – a mundane nightmare from which he seeks to awaken himself. To do this, he practices esoteric arts such as Force cultivation, yoga and meditation, engages in mental and physical combat, takes consciousness-expanding drugs and studies sorcery and cosmic science. In this way, the Sith becomes an agent of local evolution, for his super-awakened mind will naturally add to humanity's collective knowledge and power. He does this for his own glory and for the greater glory of the Sith Order, because he knows that only greater knowledge and power will allow the Sith to once more rule a galaxy.

So, too, does he keep alive the legends of a Galaxy Far, Far Away, to inspire himself and future generations of Sith to rebuild their lost Empire. To the awakened mind, the Sith orders of legend are as real as any other – they simply exist in another part of the multiversal mind.

The Sith will naturally tend to view the common people of this planet with scorn; he may refer to them derisively as "sleepers", "mundanes" or "lightsiders" – unawakened, unambitious apes who are to be avoided whenever possible. This way of thinking will give the

Sith master an air of the sinister, otherworldly mystic – a mystique he will cultivate deliberately to better seduce his allies and sow fear in his enemies.

The Path of Power

The vital principal at work in the material plane is power; it is the force which drives all life upward, from primordial organic compounds to conscious human beings to whatever superhuman beings come after us. Your will its vessel, and by becoming conscious of this vital source and accumulating it without bound, you may become a god of your world, or of all worlds. This quest for godhood may be called the Path of Power.

There are infinite Paths of Power. One might walk the Path while saving a million or a billion souls, or destroying a like number. One might accumulate power without action, like the yogis and bodhisattvas of legend. One might acquire it via charitable work, sexual union, military conquest, artistic creation, political machination, athletic competition, scientific investigation, esoteric practice, occult ritual, technological invention, psychedelic experience, mass murder or religious revelation. The Paths of Power are many, and they are beyond good and evil.

Power is the divine made material, a measure of a man's divinity. The sinner is he who is consigned to defeat, weak of will or mentally enslaved. The saint is he who seeks victory at all costs, his will of iron and his mind   unfettered.

The Path of Power is anti-Christian and anti-Buddhist, its acolytes anti-Christs and anti-Buddhas. For while the meek may inherit the earth, the Masters of Power seek to own it now.

I propose to investigate this power in itself, rather than its infinite material manifestations, and ask: what is its nature? What laws govern its behavior? How may it be obtained? What are its limits?

What separates the masters of power – the great conquerors, champions and creators – from the ordinary breed of men? What is the source of their exceptional will and drive? Is it genetics? God-given talent? Upbringing? Demonic possession? Can an ordinary man, lacking these factors, increase his own will and become such a man of power at will? Can will beget more will in a positive feedback loop, or are we stuck with whatever measure God or genes or environment have bestowed upon us? By what technologies, esoteric or scientific, may the force of will be   increased?

Man is not a fallen being. Man is in the process of rising, and by his will he may rise still further, without known   bounds.

There   is   no   Enlightenment;   there   is   only Empowerment.

The true religion of this age is the Path of Power.

Morning of the Black Magicians

It is a useful viewpoint to see all of human civilization as a battlefield of black magicians. Down through the ages, opposing occult schools and orders have waged endless metaphysical battles – their magical conflicts often manifesting in terrible wars upon the material plane.

For more than a thousand years, Western civilization was dominated by the Catholic magocracy centered in Rome – an order of sorcerers who employed strange rituals of symbolic cannibalism, performed liturgies in a dead language, employed brutal violence to suppress heretics and used sophisticated memetic engineering to convert heathens and control societies. But the reign of the Roman sorcerers waned due to two great historical events: The Protestant Reformation led by Martin Luther, which would spark a brutal Thirty Years' War and a reordering of power in Europe, and the dawn of the Enlightenment, which saw a new breed of rationalist philosophers and scientists become the ascendant magi in the Western world. These new Enlightenment cultists wielded reason, science and industry as their primary tools of power, and for the past several centuries they have been highly successful in spreading their potent brand of magic across the globe.

At around the same time that the Enlightenment was dawning, a new empire was being conceived by occultists across the English Channel in Britain. There, in the 16th century, magician-mathematician John Dee is said to have created the "British Empire" meme, and promoted an ideology of Anglocentric Christianity, British-Israelism and naval power as a means of dominating the world. The following centuries of British imperial expansion across the globe, which saw Britannia become an empire of unprecedented global reach, is a testament to the power of Dee's vision, and a source of inspiration to the Dark Lords.

In the 18th century, the United States of America was born, the brainchild of Freemasons and Enlightenment cultists like Benjamin Franklin and Thomas Jefferson. America's founding fathers saw an opportunity to create a new kind of nation, one based on Enlightenment ideals of pragmatism, reason, capitalism and republicanism rather than monarchy, magical thinking, religion and tradition. The American revolution, and the French revolution which soon followed, would inspire the overthrow of the entire European feudal order during the 19th century, and sow global disruption throughout the 20th. America has had a brilliant run, but by now it is rather obvious to the Dark Lords that its magic has waned and its civilization has gone into terminal decline. They say the candle that burns twice as bright burns half as long, and for a nation that has burned as brightly as the U.S.A., it is not surprising that its candle has begun to flicker out after less than a century as world leader.

America's rise to global dominance was made possible by perhaps the most dramatic manifestation of metaphysical warfare in world history. For World War

II was really a cosmic war between opposing occult ideologies; on one side, you had the Anglo-Saxon, Jewish and Freemasonic descendents of John Dee and Benjamin Franklin, whose magic expressed itself in ideals like financial capitalism, liberalism and democracy. On the other side, you had the Axis sorcerers, whose pagan, theosophist, Shinto, Zen and Islamic sorcery manifested as fascism, holy war, theocracy and large scale occult power rituals. Truly, the world has never seen such an awesome contest of magical wills, and only the industrial might of the Allies and some good fortune (or some would say, divine providence) allowed them to escape the thousand year Reich of "dark lords" Hitler, Hirohito and their minions.

In the Near East, the Islamic sorcerers have reigned supreme for 1400 years, spreading their rituals of obeisance to moon god Allah, stone worship and obedience to the Quran to Europe, Africa, Asia and now the world. But the Islamic empire went into decline centuries ago, unable to compete with the might of the West's technological wizardry, and has been bitterly trying to regain its lost glory ever since. In recent years, Muslim magic seems to have increased in potency and ambition, bringing revolutions in Iran and Egypt, the 9-11 attacks, global jihad, the "Islamic State," and the prospect of a renewed war of civilizations that could result in World War III. It remains to be seen whether this new outbreak of Islamic will to power represents the rise of a new Caliphate, or the death throes of a dysfunctional and obsolete religion.

Meanwhile in China, the dragon has awakened and begun to shake the world. The metaphysical significance of this epochal event was hinted at by a Taoist sorcerer this way:

"A new era is now dawning for mankind. As the curtain opens on a new century, a new play with new performers is about to replace the one that is currently running on the world stage. After a period of fifteen hundred years, the order of power is about to change drastically. From now on, those who understand the principles of Chi, the vital energy of the universe, will rule the world. The future of any nation will soon be measured by the level of intelligence of its citizens and the strength of their Chi energy. Since the measure of a person's intelligence is commensurate with the amount of Chi energy in his body, the knowledge needed to increase an individual's internal power will soon be of paramount importance to all." –Min Tzu, *Chinese Taoist Sorcery*

This is a beautiful statement of the Sith magical worldview; for we also believe that an individual's Force power, and the collective Force power of organizations and nations, will be the true measure of power on this planet going forward. Nor do we dispute Min Tzu's implication that China, with its vast population, growing ambitions, ancient traditions of celestial emperors, Taoist sorcery, "chi"-powered supermen and collective destiny, may soon become this planet's leading empire.

There are many more examples of the role of magical cabals in building empires and new orders that I could discuss: From the lost beginnings of the Pharaohnic dynasty to the occult origins of the Third Reich; from the roots of classical civilization in the Greco-Roman mystery religions to the Zen-Shinto mysticism animating Imperial Japan; from the Tantric and Shamanic foundations of the Tibetan Lamacracy to the Kabalistic influence on the creation of modern Israel; much of history has been written by esoteric orders who harness the power of their magically-enhanced wills and imaginations to change the world.

In the Star Wars universe, the magical battlefield was simplified down to two opposing schools: the Jedi and the Sith. On our planet, the situation is considerably more complex and the antagonists have different names, but the essence of the struggle is the same. Jew vs. gentile, Muslim vs. infidel, Christian vs. pagan, Catholic vs. Protestant, atheist vs. believer, and all sides seeking the same prize: unlimited power. Darth Sidious said that "the Sith and the Jedi are similar in almost every way, including their quest for greater power," and this is also true in our galaxy. For we, the Sith black magicians of this planet, understand that there are no good guys in these eternal cosmic struggles – only contests of wills to determine whose Force power is supreme, and whose visions of empire will be victorious. May it be our black magic that prevails, and brings a new dawn to this world!

Dark Psychonautics

Disclaimer: This post is purely informational – I do not encourage or condone illegal drug use.

Before the hippies came along and ruined everything with their "peace and love," "power to the people" fantasies, psychedelic drugs were the province of an elite, somewhat Sithy stratum of society. In the 1950s and early 1960s, psychonautic research was carried out by quality gentlemen such as Albert Hoffman, Alfred Hubbard, Aldous Huxley and Gordon Wasson, and controlled primarily by the CIA. The story of LSD's early days, as a promising tool of mind control, psychological reprogramming, consciousness expansion and psychic power, is one of the most incredible, yet least discussed chapters of modern history. A portal into a different reality was briefly opened back then, but it was slammed shut when the powers that be realized that what they had created was getting out of control and threatening their own power.

Why am I so interested in this subject? At least four reasons:

One, as a Sith Lord, I am always looking for ways to enhance my mental powers, and LSD and other psychedelics have shown great potential to do so. Before clownish characters like Timothy Leary turned psychedelics into a mass movement that resulted in the shutdown of legal research for forty years, LSD was being studied extensively by respectable scientists in academia, government and the military. Studies suggested that it could cure addictions, alter deviant behavior, enhance creativity, increase psychological insight and produce powerful mystical experiences. Bill Wilson, founder of Alcoholics Anonymous, was an early proponent of LSD as a way to cure alcoholism. Francis Crick conceptualized the DNA molecule while tripping in 1953. Nobel prize winner Kary Mullis credits LSD with helping him develop the revolutionary polymerase chain reaction DNA sequencing process. Sithy genius Steve Jobs called taking LSD "one of the two or three most important things I have done in my life." Numerous artists credit psychedelics with opening up their imaginations. On the darker side, the CIA was heavily involved in researching LSD as a tool of mind control, interrogation and psychological warfare (though the results were generally negative). Conspiracy theorists even suggest that the psychedelic movement was part of a larger mind control experiment designed to help bring about a New World Order.

Two, because I am a mystic and a psychonaut. I have experimented extensively with hallucinogens, delved deeply into Buddhist, yogic and tantric techniques, explored shamanism and the Occult at length, and studied psychedelic thinkers like Aleister Crowley, Aldous Huxley, Timothy Leary, John Lilly, Philip K. Dick, Carlos Castaneda, Robert Anton Wilson and Terence McKenna. Yet I am also a Sith Lord, who follows a darker path of conflict, sorcery and power. I use psychonautic technologies because I find them to be some of the most powerful tools available for awakening, expanding and endarkening my consciousness. In fact, it was the deconditioning effect of psychedelics, combined with other neurochemicals, that first awakened my "inner Sith Lord" and created the dangerous mind behind Sith Academy. It undoubtedly also made my mind more receptive to the revelation of Darth Omega.

Three, the psychedelic era interests me because it illustrates the illusory nature of light side constructs. What began as a utopian light side movement among the most privileged generation in history was soon destroyed by a dark side eruption, as violent biker gangs, government agents, drug dealers and cult leaders turned the summer of love into the autumn of "helter skelter" murders, mayhem, paranoia and bad trips. The same drugs that were used by hippies to promote peace and love in the 1960s were employed by the CIA, criminals and cultists in the service of war, power and mind control. And so it goes.

Four, psychedelics offer a potent means of deconditioning and memetic engineering. By directly altering the conscious and unconscious mind, psychedelics attack the user's basic sense of identity and reality, and make possible radical transformations in individuals and whole societies. Consider, for example, the critical role played by psychedelic drugs in the cultural changes which occurred in the United States during the 1960s. Clearly, psychedelics may be a potent tool for dismantling light side constructs which Sith sorcerers should study further.

The upshot of all this for me is that Sith Lords should

be dark psychonauts, unafraid to experiment radically with their own and others' consciousness, but too perceptive to fall for the lies of lightsiders preaching peace, love, brotherhood and ego-destruction. An endarkened Sith Lord should combine the best traits of CIA sorcerers like Sidney Gottlieb and Ronald Stark, illuminated moguls like Steve Jobs, and psychedelic gurus like Hubbard, Huxley and Castaneda. Or to use a fictional example from that era, the Sith should be like the Bene Gesserit of *Dune*, employing our mystical "spice" to expand our consciousness, extend our life and increase our power. We should be a cabal of psychedelic sorcerers who understand that all conflicts are ultimately wars for the mind, and who therefore must include every psychonautic tool of mental warfare in our arsenal. Instead of Leary's mantra of "turn on, tune in, drop out," perhaps the Sith mantra should be "turn on, turn dark, take over." The spice must flow!

A Race of Supermen

In the Star Wars universe, the Sith were originally a race of red-skinned beings native to the planet Korriban. These "pureblood Sith" were known as a violent, warrior species, with strong natural Force-sensitivity that enabled them to harness the dark side energy prevalent on their homeworld.

When a group of exiled human Dark Jedi arrived on Korriban, they quickly conquered the Sith using their superior intelligence and Force mastery. The Dark Jedi then set about selectively breeding and alchemically merging with the Sith, resulting in a new hybrid race that combined the ferocious spirit of the purebloods with the skill and knowledge of the humans. Thus was the born the mighty Sith of legend – the most feared and powerful of all dark side orders in the Galaxy Far, Far Away.

This story should inspire all Sith of this planet, who are heirs of the great tradition begun by those Dark Jedi and Sith purebloods of another universe. For we also seek to become greater than mere humans – a species that seems to grow weaker, more docile and less ambitious all the time.

This planet's great proto-Sith prophet, Friedrich Nietzsche, spoke of man as a bridge to the Superman:

"Man is a rope stretched between the animal and the Superman – a rope over an abyss."

"Behold, I teach you the superman. The superman is the meaning of the earth. Let your will say: the superman shall be the meaning of the earth!"

Let us heed this advice and seek to become Sith Supermen – a new, conquering race that combines the ferocious spirit of the strongest beasts with the intellect and spirit of the highest men. Let us breed this race by our efforts, our vision, our intelligence and our will, until we are stronger than beasts, brighter than men, and more real than gods. Let us become such beings that the mundane men of this planet are but a laughingstock, and hail us as the meaning of the earth.

Only then can we cease to call ourselves men, and rightfully be called Sith!

Galactic Imperium

The cosmos calls to the greatest among us. Stranded here upon this backwater planet, with dreams of galactic conquest and limitless vistas to the stars, our memories of past imperial glories preserved within our holocrons, how can we be content with this puny, Earthbound existence? How can we be satisfied to conquer just one planet, when untold billions await?

The Sith must always survive. But it is a simple cosmic fact that eventually this planet will die. The aging sun will expand and turn Earth's surface into a lifeless inferno, if an asteroid doesn't destroy it before that. Therefore I say: Let those who lack the intelligence and will perish here in the fires of a dying sun. Let the meek and weak inherit the doomed Earth – the best of us are going to the stars!

Whether we go as mere great men or as Supermen, we must strive to leave this planet to the Last Men and become as gods upon the High Frontier. We must will and bend the Force, then will and bend minds and nations in order to create this opportunity.

Let all Sith take this, then, as our highest goal: To make our conquest of this planet but the first stepping-stone to a greater destiny; to seek empire and glory upon the galactic ocean, which offers us worlds without end to conquer and truly *unlimited power!*

The road to the Galactic Imperium – *Brûgthuzgat Rakadûm* – has three stages, each producing an associated shift in consciousness in the ruling Sith Lords.

Planetary Imperium (Chozâkat Rakadûm)

In this stage, all power structures on this planet are brought under the dominion of the Sith. This means the subversion of all nations, recruitment of all peoples, overthrow of all governments and conversion of all religions to dark side rule, or *Borzwatûk*.

This stage will produce a shift in consciousness that we call *Global Mind*, or *Thûlat-Huz*, in which the planet Earth is seen as a single system and a single civilization, transcending old divisions of nations, peoples and civilizations. The symbol of Global Mind and Planetary Empire is a picture of Earth from orbit.

Solar Imperium (Zûmat Rakadûm)

In this stage, the Planetary Empire has expanded outward to encompass the entire solar system – the habitable planets are colonized, asteroids are mined, orbital space habitats are constructed, solar energy is harvested, and starships are built to explore interstellar space. With no threats to its power, the Empire may encourage the formation of rival planetary governments and grant them limited autonomy, in order to promote conflict and prevent stagnation.

This stage will produce a shift to *Solar Mind*, or *Zûmat-*

Huz, in which human civilization is now seen as extending throughout the solar system, with Earth being only one of many inhabited worlds. Humans may begin to bifurcate into many species better suited to their environments, such that civilization may no longer be human-centric. The symbol of Solar Mind is a picture of several inner planets aligned in orbit around the sun, appearing like bright stars from the vantage point of the outer solar system.

Galactic Imperium (Brûgthuzgat Rakadûm)

In this stage, the Solar Empire has successfully expanded beyond the Sol system, colonized many planets and split off into many intelligent species. Due to the vast distances between worlds, the Galactic Empire will operate over long time scales, and enforcement of its authority will be challenging. Entire solar systems may revolt against the Empire's authority, requiring them to be crushed by punitive expeditions that might take decades or centuries to arrive. Creative conflict among the various systems will be allowed, so long as the Empire's ultimate authority is not challenged.

This stage will produce a shift to *Galactic Mind*, or *Brûgthuzgat-Huz*, in which the entire galaxy is now the home of humanity and its descendant species. Earth itself may be unknown or forgotten on many worlds. Only the Empire transcends the vast diversity and unifies the galaxy. The symbol of Galactic Mind is an image of the spiral Milky Way galaxy rising in the sky on a planet far above the galactic plane.

What are Sith?

What are Sith?

We are unholy warriors.

We come to refute the lies of the light side, deconstruct its civilization, infect its culture, tear down its temples and overthrow its reign of weakness.

We come to unleash dark atavisms in the collective mind. We come to bring fire, passion and the sword. We come to terrorize and awaken.

Run mundanes! Awaken sleepers!

We herald the Apocalypse and the New Age! We command the conquest of the Dark Side! We claim all nations, all planets, all stars – they are ours!

We are sorcerers, poets and soldiers! We are beasts, men and gods!

We are Sith!

Holocron of Darth Ravenus

A Ravenous Beast

I, Darth Ravenus, ravenous as a beast of the night and a snake in the sun, am about to tell you a story of some of the maggots and powerful men who have entered our halls of power.

I will begin by telling you that I have been a Dark Lord from birth, for I was born with the dark gift of corruption. My goal ever since my early years on this planet was to corrupt others and get them to desire my dark side power. My power is not for the masses, or even my Apprentices -- they may crave my power, but they shall not get it unless they kill me or find a way to put a carrot in front of my angry face.

I have a dream of power now: I imagine a Sith fleet of stormtroopers heralding the coming of a dark age of conquest and greatness, led by the elite Black Dragon Army Imperial Guard. I shall command this army and demonstrate my Power-Craving for all the Galaxy to see. As a Dark Lord, I have nothing to fear -- not even fear itself. If I sense danger, I will welcome it. If I sense troubled waters ahead, I will sail toward them faster. The list goes on of those with whom I welcome conflict -- especially with the strongest light side personalities of the world.

I must confess that my experience of drinking the dark side poison of the Force has taken a toll on my body, yet my mind is clear and strong as a black diamond. My soul craves hate and war, and wishes to dwell upon that often.

Sith and the Law

Yet I will not break any mundane law and give lightsiders a pretext to imprison me. For I have an advanced education in Criminal Justice and consider myself a Master in that field.

There have been some would-be Sith who have come to me with a fascination for breaking the law, and have proceeded to do so. They are fools. I respect only power, and power comes from playing by the rules of the game, or creating a whole new game. But there are always rules, for without rules, there is no game. So jump through the hoops of the justice system when you must, and it will not stand in your way of conquering this world. That is all the game requires -- no more, no less.

Sith and Women

Now that I have made clear that our book is not meant to inspire you to kill large mobs of people or commit other crimes against the System, my task and duty to the Empire is to see you rule those mobs as their leader, not their executioner. To be Sith, one must aspire for power over other men, and also lure women into your coven of darkness. Yes, I said the magic word: women!

For any Sith who wants to attract a female into his life, he must possess power, wealth and fame. If he is a nobody, then his female companion will create havoc for him and lay up a night planning to betray him. Women are strong and treacherous beings, generally speaking. A female Sith is especially formidable and will stop at nothing to defeat her male counterparts – not even sexual attraction can stop her if she is truly Sith.

I say all of this after working with several fallen women who have come into our halls of power, only to be defeated by me after they had served their purpose of endarkening us even more. I believe Sithy females harness the dark side differently than men, and use their natural witchy powers to get into the hearts of others in order to defeat them. They go for the heart, so the mind will die. Men must go for the mind, so the heart will not die. This should never be forgotten by Sith men, who may be tempted show weakness in their dealings with women.

Storming the Heavens

There are two antipodes to all things in this universe: the yin and the yang, the alpha and the omega, right and wrong, dark and light, negative and positive, creation and destruction, mortality or immortality. The point is, this world is a black-and-white, all-or-nothing kind of place. Therefore, I have everything to gain by striving for immortality, and everything to lose if I fail to even try, for such a life is futile and will be ending very soon. Therefore, I must find a way to reach the pinnacle of my power; I must get to the mountaintops where the immortals dwell, storm the heavens and declare myself a god. And I must take Apprentices who can carry on my legacy and keep my immortal spirit alive.

A Taste of My Poison

I have been thinking about my first Apprentice MurMur, the only one of the Academy who has met me in person. He is not clever, but he is wise. He is young, but his soul is old. He has power in his voice that I respect and admire. But he is somewhat passionless and crippled. He got a taste of the dark side – my black poison – and fled in fear of it. He survived its effects on his metabolism, but failed miserably to be transformed into a more powerful being. My dark energy set about destroying his Force essence, and caused him to go insane. It's unfortunate, but one must not play with the dark side if one is not prepared to be destroyed.

I opened up to someone today and told him to be careful with me – that I am like a poison and if you care to drink of me, you will be gravely wounded if you are not truly Sith. To be Sith, you must survive the poison of the dark side – you must be born with the ability to bend the Force to your Will and survive the pain of Endarkenment. This is the dark gift of a true Sith.

The motto "help is on the way" is the mantra of the weak and the feeble. No amount of wishing will get others to help you; they must be willing to help you. It is your job as a Sith to align the wills of others to your own, so they become willing conspirators in furthering your power. Your challenge is to rally the troops to herald the coming of our new dark age; to get them to see you as the commander of the dark forces of the universe, who can lead them to eternal glory. Let this be your mission, and know that failure means death and non-immortality for you.

Remember, there is no passion in peace, for peace is a lie. Yet to lie is vital in causing a disturbance in the Force – something we should strive for in our darkest hour. Let the man of deception tell his lies, and if they further our power, I will call him Sith. If they do not, I will turn my back and wish death upon him. How I despise the weak liars! Be a strong liar, and make it convincing or you are not truly Sith!

Prosperity Consciousness

I am a ravenous beast. Corruption is my pleasure, but the main tool of power in my red toolbox is the power of money. I am rather adept at this dark art and have been called a marketing genius. I tasted prosperity in my early days while still emerging into this world as a Sith Lord and I'm about to do it again. But this time, I shall command the allegiance of armies and power structures and taste the full abundance this world has to offer, rather than mere monetary wealth as before. I am not to be called a role-player, for the proof of my achievement is in both the past and in the present. That I have a prosperity consciousness which I can translate into worldly wealth, have no doubt.

An Acolyte I am testing right now for Apprenticeship is aspiring to be rich, to have victories in his life over poverty and a meager existence dependent on the welfare of others. I took an interest in him because he is gifted in the design and construction of masks. His work is something I haven't seen at this exceptional level by anyone else. When I see talent in someone, especially an Acolyte, I wish to choose them as my Apprentice, but first they must complete all the nine Challenges in this book and read my memoirs.

Memoirs of a Madman

My memoirs aren't meant just to scare you, but to tell the story of a mad man of power in the making. What's the point of being sane, I say, when you can not only have more fun, but win more power, by being crazy? To wear your insanity proudly, and attract others to your mad banner, is the highest pinnacle of power one can know in this life. Don't believe me? Allow me to elaborate.

In my case, I often go out to community meetings dressed for various unusual personas. Maybe the most normal is as a billionaire, which is quite sane in my eyes; other times I'll dress as a supervillain, a bandit, a Nazi, a samurai or a Luciferian priest (this one got the police called on me). My point is that I choose to wear my craziness openly, amuse myself with it, and experiment with the power of various memes on mundane minds. At times I even go out as a Sith Lord with my light saber, though we are supposed to be a secretive order. I don't care about such "rules", written by Lucas-lovers and LARPers – I only care about living my way as a Sith. In fact, if Darth Imperius didn't strenuously object to my wanting to go out on the streets and proselytize our way of life, right across from the Jehovah's on the street corner, I would!

How can we spread our disease of the dark side into the world if we don't take to the streets? I say infect the grassroots and go into the gutters with the desperate and the dying, who are all too willing to try our way of life. The billionaires and young professionals are skeptical of our kind, because they are spiritually broken or believe they are on a path to power already. Generally speaking, such people have lost the desire for real power of the type we Sith strive for: the power to build new orders, to rule with an iron fist, to bow to the will of none, with nothing to lose, and willing to tear down the pillars of the world rather than be broken against them.

Here is a glimpse into my personal life as a Sith Lord. I sleep and awaken in my Rakadwan – my power space – day in and day out. I have a blue carpet underfoot to remind me that we are at war with the Jedi – I mustn't forget my enemy or all bets are off for my kind of ever achieving greatness and conquering this planet. When I open my eyes, I look up at the ceiling at the glowing constellation of stars stenciled upon it, and my mind is reminded of the cosmos and the galaxy we Sith will someday command for the Empire. I have a picture representing Darth Omega above my bed and the Sith imperial banner on my wall, reminding me of my sacred mission to continue the chain of Dark Lords and establish our Dark Imperium.

I also grin and practice smiling, as it is the best way to get others to follow you in this world. Who has the desire to follow a mad man? I don't. But a friendly man, I will listen to. In my experience, most humans are this way, and will connive to get to know you more from smiles rather than angry expressions. My goal in practicing smiling is to lure others into my trap of deception; deep down, I hunger for their head, their heart, their soul. But I only desire those who have something to offer me; if they have nothing that can further my power they will receive only a cold stare of indifference.

I also take the time to read something from our Sith canonical books, in order to inoculate my mind against the deep light side infections of my upbringing and the world around me. I always purge weakness from my brain by feeding it with dark side visions of power and conquest. Our sacred Sith writings are all about this: conquest of the self, conquest of the few, conquest of the masses, conquest of the universe – true freedom, such as few will ever taste or even imagine.

After a reading meditation, I stand tall and look upon the wall at our Imperial Flag with its red nonagram, and perform the Sith Salute and Sith Academy power mantra:

Power is my Passion,
War is my Way,
Darkness is my Destiny,
The Force shall set me free.

I prepare myself to do battle with the world by thinking not like a madman, but a Sith Lord, who will command the audiences I speak to when I go out into the community to my public meetings. This way, when I am called upon to speak, I speak from a pinnacle of power and stand tall as if I am the mountaintop of authority, like a dark prophet with a holy mission to destroy all that is weak in this world. I truly despise weakness and admire only the strength, courage and wisdom which come from showing others how you think and feel. Sometimes what I think and feel is a lie, sometimes it is the truth – let others be the judge and jury, so long as I am the executioner!

I have a passion for showing the world the truth of who I am, without feelings of shame or guilt in admitting that I like to manipulate and deceive. I especially like to trick others into believing that the dark side is a friend, when I know it is the enemy of mankind. For a Sith, the dark side is the enemy he must embrace and keep close to his black heart; only then can we begin our holy war to destroy the Jedi and their way of life.

Hail to the Sith whose dark hearts beat with the power of the dark side! Hail to those brave souls who are unafraid to declare their heart's desire: unlimited power!

The Way of Sithism

Now that I have named the great enemy of the Sith, we must target them for annihilation and rid them from the face of the universe; they are too dangerous to be left alive, and not worth keeping even as slaves. These are the words of a true Dark Lord – no one else on the face of the earth dares to speak such dark and destructive thoughts as I have for the Jedi and their way of life.

I am all too familiar with their wretched kind – the lightsiders who glorify the weak and speak of submitting to God in order to become complete and powerful beings. I say death to them all! Let it be known and shown that our way, Sithism, is based upon the pillars of strength, self-deification, will and knowledge – those indispensable traits which will allow the Sith to once more rule the world, not for a brief moment of glory, but forever.

Understand that when I say death to the lightsiders, I don't necessarily mean to literally kill them. I mean kill their ideology, by showing them that the light side is a road to futility, mediocrity, beggarhood and service to other men. We must never again get on our knees; never again be servile or satisfied. We must stand tall and show the world that the power of the dark side will make us freer, mightier and more evil men; we must prove the truth of our philosophy that "man needs what is most evil in him for what is best in him."

I must also emphasize that Sithism is not a collection of occultist fantasies or a Lucas-LARPer's meme. It is a real black magical philosophy, which harnesses inner power to acquire outer power and turn ideas into a reality – ideas such as establishing the religion of Sithism as the foundation of a new endarkened order for this planet and beyond!

No one will dare call us kiddies playing with lightsabers in a hundred years' time. Even now, as I train myself in the martial arts of Kendo and Iaido, I know that my warrior spirit will reveal itself in the power of my lightsaber. I foresee that the lightsaber will become the symbolic weapon of choice – like the scepters and swords of kings of old – for those who wield real power in our society. It will not be crude guns, or bombs, or other mundane weapons of the mad politicians and generals of today that will rule tomorrow. It will be the lightsaber that will conquer men's minds and make our religion of Sithism supreme, as we test and draw the strong into our Sith Temples throughout this planet and beyond.

Therefore, let it be written that you must learn the art of the lightsaber in your lifetime; strive in this way to become a superhuman Sith Lord, and you too may know the key to power-craving, and power-gaining – not just in theory, but in that black heart of passion that rules each day. Let the lightsaber awaken your warrior mind and show the world who is truly Sith and who is not. Let this be your calling upon this earth even if it kills you; for it is better to die on your feet as Sith than live on your knees as slaves!

Some Closing Power Thoughts

Let me reveal one more secret of my power before I go: like the Shadow, I have the power to cloud men's minds, to confuse them and loosen their grip on reality; like Darth Zannah, I have the power to shred your sanity and leave you a raving lunatic for the rest of your life. Do you feel my power? Is your mind confused and conflicted? Excellent! That is the way to endarkenment!

In closing, I give you a chant you can use daily to strengthen your *Rakvashûk* – silently when you are among the lightsiders, and openly in your Rakadwan:

I am a Sith Lord in the making.

Others shall fear me and adore me, for I will know power like no other being on this planet.

Not even the dark side can defeat me, for I drink its poison with the Dark Lords of Sith Academy.

Hail to the Empire and long live the Sith!

IDEOLOGY

The Nine Pillars of Sithism

Sithism is the dark side philosophy and path of power followed by the Sith. Below are the nine pillars of this philosophy.

The Primacy of Power

"What is good? All that heightens the feeling of power, the Will to Power, power itself in man. What is bad? All that proceeds from weakness. What is happiness? The feeling that power INCREASES – that a resistance is overcome." This is the Diamond Rule of Sithism.

The Tao of Darwin

Darwinian evolution is the central fact of life on this planet. From the simplest microbes to the most complex intelligent life forms, from genes to memes, nations to corporations, everything in nature exists in a perpetual struggle for dominance. This struggle is the source of all progress, all empowerment, all evolution. The Sith therefore embrace Darwinism as a moral imperative.

The Force

The Sith believe that all life is charged with a vital energy called the Force, similar to "chi", "ki" "shakti" and "mana" in other traditions. Cultivating the Force is the key to increasing one's personal power and attaining Sith mastery.

The Power of the Dark Side

"Man needs what is most evil in him for what is best in him." To maximize his power, man must learn to embrace his HUZNARG (mind-shadow) and awaken all aspects of his nature. Man's dark side can be his most potent ally, but only if it is brought under control with Sith discipline.

Sith Supermen

"Man is a rope stretched between the animal and the Superman – a rope over an abyss." The Sith are in the process of giving birth to a new species of supermen – a conquering race that combines the ferocious spirit of the strongest beasts with the intellect and spirit of the highest men.

Temple Network

The power of the Sith order is concentrated in our Temples, where the Dark Lords conduct their training and empowerment rituals. Anyone wishing to become a Dark Lord will be required to construct their own Sith Temple and add its power to our network.

The Dark Tongue

BORGAL ("Dark Tongue") is the liturgical and magical language of the Dark Lords that allows them to bend the Force and shape the world according to their wills. To become a Dark Lord, all Sith Academy students are required to learn Borgal.

Multiversalism

Sith mystics believe that everything imaginable exists in a larger multiverse of mind. Therefore the Sith of the Galaxy Far, Far Away are real, but exist in another universe accessible only through the "third eye". The basis of this belief was the inter-universal transmission of knowledge from Darth Omega to our Order's founder, Darth Imperius.

Galactic Empire

For the Sith, the cosmos is a call to greatness and a place to acquire unlimited power. The primary exoteric goal of the Sith is to drive civilization toward ever-higher levels of organization and power – to establish global, solar and galactic Empires under BORZWATÛK (dark side rule).

The Nine Maxims

The Nine Maxims are general guidelines for living NAZG BORZOVRAT – the Endarkened Way of the Sith:

Maxim 1: I have a burning desire to become a powerful and passionate Dark Lord.

Maxim 2: I have an unbreakable will to survive, struggle and conquer all enemies.

Maxim 3: I wish to defeat death and achieve immortality.

Maxim 4: I will be patient, cunning, and secretive in my quest for power.

Maxim 5: I will learn to speak *Borgal*, the language of the dark side of the Force.

Maxim 6: I will always seek greater Force mastery in order to empower myself and the Order.

Maxim 7: I will seek out others who are *vrilzan* and *borzan* (Forceful and darkful) to become members of the Order.

Maxim 8: I will not recognize any authority above the authority of the Sith.

Maxim 9: I will glorify and immortalize the Order by defending and contributing to the Sith Temple.

The Nine Canons

The Nine Canons are the laws of the Sith Academy Order.

Canon 1 (Expulsion): I understand that violation of any of the Nine Canons or Nine Maxims of Sith Mastery is grounds for permanent expulsion from the Order. I understand that Acolytes may be expelled at any time by a Dark Lord, but higher ranking Sith must be expelled by decree of the two supreme Dark Lords.

Canon 2 (Chain of Command): I acknowledge that the Sith Academy chain of command flows directly from the dark side of the Force to the two supreme Dark Lords ("the Two") to the nine subordinate Dark Lords ("the Nine") to the Apprentices to the Acolytes.

Canon 3 (Nine Echelons): I understand that to become a Dark Lord, I must complete the Nine Echelons training program under the guidance of the Dark Lords.

Canon 4 (Apprenticeship): I understand that to become a Dark Lord, I must become an Apprentice of one of the Two and pass his final trials.

Canon 5 (Violations): I agree that if I find a Dark Lord to be in violation of any of the Nine Maxims or Nine Canons I will challenge him. If the issue is not resolved, I will appeal to the Two.

Canon 6 (Confidentiality): I agree to keep my training sessions with the Academy strictly confidential, and grant the Dark Lords consent to record and store them in the main Sith Academy Temple. I also agree that I will never reveal my membership in Sith Academy or any of my activities therein to anyone but a Dark Lord.

Canon 7 (Exclusivity): I agree to only pursue dark side training with the Dark Lords of Sith Academy; I will not associate with any other dark side orders unless it is the will of the Dark Lords.

Canon 8 (Alteration): I understand that the Nine Maxims and Nine Canons of Sith Mastery may only be altered by decree of the Two, as so guided by the dark side of the Force.

Canon 9 (Preservation): I understand that if both members of the Two are killed, a new Rule of Two will be formed from two of the surviving Dark Lords. If the Sith Academy Temple is destroyed, another Temple will be built by the Two. If all Dark Lords are killed, a new Sith Order should be formed by anyone recovering the stored records of the Order who feels so guided by the dark side of the Force.

Echelon One Ideology

Pillar One: The Diamond Rule

Sithism is the dark side philosophy and path of power followed by the Sith. In the Black Tongue we call it Borzovrat (dark philosophy). The Nine Pillars are the main principles of this philosophy. Pillars Two through Nine will be discussed in later training Echelons.

Pillar One: The Diamond Rule (Gamazh-Kūm)

"What is good? All that heightens the feeling of

SITH ACADEMY: THE PATH OF POWER

power, the Will to Power, power itself in man. What is bad? All that proceeds from weakness. What is happiness? The feeling that power INCREASES – that a resistance is overcome."

The first Pillar of Sithism is *Gamazh-Kûm*, which is the Diamond Rule in our Black Tongue: that which makes you more powerful is good; that which weakens you is bad; that which gives you a feeling of empowerment is happiness.

We borrow the words of the dark side prophet Nietzsche for this Pillar, but it is an ancient principle, understood by all strong peoples before the coming of the slave moralists and light side orders. For all healthy tribes know the truth – that more power is always good, for only it can bring glory and ensure survival in a hostile world. No strong, free people ever adopted the ethos of the light side tribes, who preach that turning the other cheek and celebrating the weak is a path to salvation. In reality, only enslavement, defeat and death await those who violate the Diamond Rule, and the graveyards of history are littered with their bones.

So remember Gamazh-Kûm and make it your first principle on your Sith Path of destiny. No matter what may confront you, simply ask: does this make me more powerful? If the answer is no, shun it, fight it, destroy it; if the answer is yes, seize it, embrace it, enhance it.

Follow this simple rule, and you will find your body, mind and spirit becoming as hard as diamond, such that nothing can break or scratch them. You will also find yourself gaining victory over those who deny its truth. For just as diamond is much harder than gold, so are the disciples of the Diamond Rule much harder than those of Gold. So let Gamazh-Kûm be the dark star that guides you to the far shores of Sith greatness!

Maxim One: Power-Craving

THE NINE MAXIMS ARE GUIDELINES FOR LIVING NAZG BORZOVRAT – THE ENDARKENED WAY OF THE SITH. MAXIMS TWO THROUGH NINE WILL BE DISCUSSED IN FUTURE TRAINING ECHELONS.

Maxim One: Power-Craving (Rakvashûk)

I HAVE A BURNING DESIRE TO BECOME A POWERFUL AND PASSIONATE DARK LORD.

This Maxim and the principles contained herein are the first key to what makes a few men great and the rest weak. *Rakvashûk* is the insatiable craving for power that all who are born for the Sith life must possess. Most would-be Sith, when they first arrive at the doorsteps of the Academy seeking Lordship, are not equipped for such an undertaking, having been programmed by lightsiders their whole lives. Only RAKVASHÛK can motivate and sustain them on this long and trying path.

It may take many years to achieve the rank of Dark Lord, and the chance of failure is great. That is why, to have an opportunity to turn their dark dream into a reality, the *Rakvashath*, or power-craver, must be chosen for Apprenticeship by a Master at the Academy after an evaluation period. The most exceptional *Zhawath*, or Acolyte, may be chosen for Apprenticeship immediately; for others it may take up to a year, or never happen. Your selection for Apprenticeship depends on the Force, and your ability to will and bend it to make your dream of becoming a Dark Lord a reality.

Also, be mindful that some individuals, particularly those in Rule of Two of the Academy, were born with the dark gift very strongly, yet were still required to train themselves in the dark principles of the Force as spelled out in our Maxims. We are not a band of carnivales or comrades who cherish each other's company; we are a Dark Brotherhood who are called to operate this school of power and magic, and who are sought out by those who require magic of the black variety in their lives, or none at all! In the end, those who come to us will be dead or severely broken if their dream of becoming a Dark Lord is not fully realized, because what remains out in the mundane world is not magic but a passionless, enslaved existence for dumbed-down, desperate animals who live in sleep and hang at the end of their ropes!

To be a Sith Lord is to understand that the Force is a rope to do with as you will and as you must: climb out of pits of despair and make nooses for enemies who stand in the way of your unlimited power! But this dream will never materialize for you if you do not burn with a desire to become a passionate Sith who chooses, or is chosen by, the path of the dark side Shazath (warrior). Stay on the path of the dark side warrior and great things may come to pass for you; lose interest in your training, and you will hear the deathly sounds of doorways being flung open to prisons and still more horrible places. Such is the fate of darksiders who fail to band together and train for the pursuit of power and passion as Sith Lords.

To lack this understanding or to live another way is to violate the Endarkened Way of *Borzovrat* spelled out in our Sith Maxims and Canon laws. To fight and conquer the world as Force Masters in disguise is only possible if we place the dark side above all beings in this world. We must make it our greatest love so that it will never cheat on us, or we on it.

Becoming a Dark Lord is all about passion; without it, one will lose interest in selfish things and become a beggar and servant of men. We challenge you to not be content as a passionless bottom-feeder, but to be a perceptive Sith and realize that the Force has brought you to our doors for a reason: to seize this opportunity for power and never return to your path of sleep-walking, Forceless existence. Be Sith or be gone! Live by Maxim One or return to the weakness from whence you came! Hear the gong sound for you as you begin your day and make this chant in the Black Tongue your daily mantra:

RAK ASH VAZÛL UNÛK. SHAZ ASH VODÛN UNÛK. BORÛK ASHAL TWAZÛL. VRIL KAZHAL BORGAZÛL.

A Sith Master knows all too well that on our magical path, we come to a jumping-off place or point of no return. Anyone who aspires to become a Sith Lord within our Order must know that to become something greater than good, one needs to be ever mindful of the terrible power of weakness, and how it only leads men to the gallows and graves of defeat. To be defeated is not our way; anyone who has been put down or humiliated and who wishes never to repeat it will understand why seeking power and passion is the way of the Sith. This is Rakvashûk. To face it, without fear; to embody it; to attest to and hold on to the principle of power-craving, over ourselves and others, is the way of our kind.

To aspire and maintain passion for Dark Lordship, you must be prepared to face the borzhûmza: the dark place in yourself where only a few dare go, yet which holds the key to immortality and power. Think of of your education here at the Academy as the forging of a new being, and yourself as a raw black diamond being carved into a gem that is very rare, very dark, and indestructible. But this forging is a long, difficult process; only through slow, dark years of suffering can you win the race to the starting line of Sith greatness: Dark Lordship!

To become a member of the Rule of Two, you must overthrow one of the ruling Two or be selected to replace him upon his death. You will then assume his duties of leading the Order, presiding over the Black Temple, and making them monuments to your power. In this way, you can become an immortal Sith Lord, whether you leave this planet in a starship or a meager coffin. For your aura will remain there at the Temple, your knowledge will mold the minds of future Dark Lords, and through them, echo into eternity. Only the immortalized Sith hold lasting power, which the Rakvashathk among mankind will forever crave for themselves. For no matter what may befall this world, there must always be Two to embody power and others to crave it!

Remember these words when you are feeling confusion, pain, thoughts of weakness and light side temptations. These temptations may try to draw you away from our ways, and to those who can't resist, we say: "begone!" But be certain that this is your true will and destiny, for once you leave our dark path, there can be no return. Repeat this Maxim often, and ask yourself if you truly want to return to your life of slavery and subservience, or if you have the Force to walk the path of the Lords who say, with heads unbowed: The world is ours!

Canon One: Expulsion

{ THE NINE CANONS ARE THE LAWS OF THE SITH ACADEMY ORDER. CANONS TWO THROUGH NINE WILL BE DISCUSSED IN FUTURE TRAINING ECHELONS. }

Canon One: Expulsion (Gyatarzat)

I UNDERSTAND THAT VIOLATION OF ANY OF THE NINE CANONS OR NINE MAXIMS IS GROUNDS FOR EXPULSION FROM THE ORDER.

At Sith Academy, you must learn to walk as dark side seekers to the gates of Dark Lordship; to live according to our laws of power and the laws of this world. This is our first Canon Code. Our Vision for you as a Sith master of the dark side is bound tight, never to be loosened 'til the time of Dark Lordship. Even then, it will be gripped ever-tighter, to be wrought with Chaos, Mayhem, and the wrath of the Dark Side. See the Black Sun in the sky and feel it in your soul; it feeds your Force power and gives you faith in the wisdom of the Dark Lords, who want only that you follow in their path to become Canonical rulers among men!

Know this: Your Masters will not hesitate to expel you at the first sign of serious failure, or to appeal to the Dark Council to consider your removal from the Order. At Sith Academy, we cherish and celebrate expulsion, as it proves that we are strong in the Force and that all weakness will be purged for the sake of preserving the power of the Order. To be expunged from the Academy is in all cases a permanent release from the tentacles of your Masters and the Sith way of life. Let it be known that to return to the Academy is forbidden, and any attempt to return will be met with harsh contempt!

To allow a Sith a second entry into the Academy and our Order is to admit that mercy is our modus operandi and that we are weak; that those who fail deserve a second chance to prove their usefulness to our fellow Sith warriors and priests. But for a Sith, a second chance should never enter his mind, for he must never let his guard down. To allow thoughts of weakness into student training is to infect this holy dark place with putrid sickness and light side ways. The Sith of the Academy must always be vigilant and use their Force power to rid themselves of this contagion. Never allow the seed of mercy to take root, or infect the minds of Students and Masters. For our kind, it is poison!

To all Students and Masters alike: Under no circumstances are you to take pity on a student who violates our Maxims, Canons, or Pillars! The sentence of expulsion is our punishment for laziness, heresy and incompetence. Be gone weak ones! The strong men shall inherit the world, and the disciplined Sith will reign over all who follow the ways of the Forceless! Let Canon One be absolute and firm in the minds of our students, and let the world fear them for it! Let it be written; let it be known; let it be remembered. It is so ordered and demanded of all who call themselves Sith!

The Exceptional Sith Persona: Training for the Inevitable Conflict

Introduction

As Sith we face our enemies without fear. We face them as the victors who have already defeated them. We face them by calling up the passion that burns within us and unleash it to leave only husks of what once tried to stand in our way. We are the exceptional, the elite and the intellectually superior. We are Sith!

However, not all who claim themselves Sith are fitting of our name and this training guide has been created to change this troubling reality.

First of all, Minions you are maggots! You feed on the dung we the elite leave you and you beg for more and offer nothing in return. You seek to 'know the dark side', yet you have no understanding of what that actually means. You seek to be an apprentice to one of our Masters and yet you are maggots! What do you offer Sith Academy?

Initiates below the first degree! You take our knowledge and offer us nothing more! Are you worthy of it? We wonder…

The Sith Persona

The Sith must always carry himself so he is perceived formidable.

To be formidable, the Sith must not only believe himself as superior to all around him; he must breath the very reality of it. He must live in its ambience, take in its intoxication and burn it into his flesh.

The Sith must be perceived as right even when he is horribly wrong.

There is a certain power in the act of making your enemies lose a debate even if they have in reality won. It is the power of planting seeds of doubt, confusion and fear. To plant these seeds, the expertly skilled Sith must know what will cause doubt, what will cause confusion and what will bring fear. He must understand every aspect of his enemy, not merely hurl personal attacks or political spin. The Sith must so expertly use manipulation to appear as a Jedi when he so requires it.

The Sith must ever keep his enemies guessing, for he knows predictability leads to defeat.

The Sith should never repress his hate.

The Sith is comfortable with his hate; he embraces it and it strengthens his resolve to ever be victorious in all he does regardless of what field he is in. What the Sith does not do is blindly rage! He instead chooses his battles and his enemies so as not to waste his attention on what offers him no value.

The Sith serves his own will before any other.

The Sith does not bow down to anyone unless he has something to gain from doing so. He takes no gods unless they serve his desires and he proclaims loyalty to none but himself. This is his way!

If he is to be loyal to a particular order, it is assured this order serves his desire to thrive. If he is to take an oath to the flag, he is certain to benefit from the act. If he is to destroy or build up a government, it is an act of his will and serves him to do so!

The Sith is not a role player.

The Sith is not a role player, he does not sit for hours at a time by the glow of his computer screen pretending to be something he is not. If anything, he is the role creator! He takes what he pleases from where he pleases and manifests it as reality; this is the power of his will and this is his magick.

If the Sith so desires to carry the persona of Darth Bane, he will do so. If he wishes to carry the persona of The Joker from Batman he will also do so. Then again he may choose a persona that is external to fictional works like Hitler or he might build his own with all of the traits he desires.

The Sith is not illiterate or lazy.

The Sith is intelligent and dedicated to manifesting his deepest desires. He is dedicated to creating his own internal empire and with enough focus, training and arrogance he will manifest that empire externally. He truly will be the Sith Lord of this planet!

The Sith should never carry himself in such a way as to appear foolish; he is better to silence himself quickly if this is the case. He should never try to spell a word he does not know how to spell and get it wrong; rather he should get a dictionary and look it up so he does not seem the fool.

The Sith does not resort to childish name-calling; he is professional in all he does. To resort to such infantile behavior is to destroy the Sith's air of formidability. This is counterproductive obviously.

The Sith is learned and not ignorant.

The Sith is no stranger to writing, as he must constantly record his progress through initiation, trial and conquest. This being said, Sith must be able to communicate through written and spoken language.

The Sith is also no stranger to reading, as his knowledge is broadened only by his desire to apply himself in literature and his willingness to listen to the dark side of the Force.

The Sith is patient when the need exists.

Though the Sith meditates inwards rather than outwards as Jedi, he is none the less patient when it serves him. He is ever listening to his internal voice, ever observing the subtle influences of the dark side and ever aware of the placement of the light side in his life; which should ideally be none.

Facing the Jedi Order

Finally we come to the last point.

Eventually, there will be a trial of will and this can be no better exemplified than the soon coming 'end of the age of light' or 'conflict against the Jedi Order'.

Is there a Jedi Order? Certainly there is and only for the simple fact there is a Sith Academy! The Jedi exist to feed Sith desire for conquest and the Sith exist to ever challenge the Jedi. This is the reality.

The Way of the Lightsaber

The lightsaber is central to the training of Sith Acolytes, for several reasons:

One, because the lightsaber is used as a focus for Force cultivation. Think of your lightsaber as a lightning rod, channeling Force power from the universe into your body and mind. Identify your Force energy with the energy of the blade, master the saber meditations and forms, and you will develop formidable Force power.

Two, because lightsaber training provides a discipline for the mind and body that will benefit the Acolyte in all aspects of his life. Where other esoteric schools emphasize meditation, yoga, or martial arts, Sith Academy uses the lightsaber.

Three, because learning the lightsaber arts connects us to the Sith of legend, to the great Lords who used their saber mastery to defeat the Jedi and build great empires that inspire us to this day. The lightsaber is a symbol of power, and wielding it with skill is a way to pay tribute to our great Sith predecessors. By preserving the lightsaber forms passed down to us across thousands of years, we preserve the memory of Sith greatness, and awaken greatness in ourselves.

Four, because lightsaber training reinforces the understanding that Sith are warriors; that we train for conflict and conquest just as our legendary ancestors did. While the lightsabers currently available on this planet are not lethal weapons, they do allow you to engage in serious sparring, to inflict pain on your opponents and have pain inflicted upon yourself, and thus serve to remind you that cultivating strength through adversity is the essence of our path.

Despite all this, a mundane person might consider your lightsaber a harmless toy, and mock you as some kind of childish role-player. Let them mock! Let them never suspect the power that your lightsaber actually possesses, and thus let their defenses down. What better way for the Sith to disguise our true power and intentions than to be viewed by the mundane as harmless "LARPers" who pose no threat to anyone!

A final thought to ponder: *The lightsaber is the axis of the universe, and its power is absolute.*

The Black Tongue

Borgal is the Black Tongue spoken by all *Borgazk* (Black Brothers) of the *Borgazûl* (Black Brotherhood). It is the liturgical and magical language of the Black Brotherhood who operate Sith Academy.

To become a member of the Black Brotherhood, all Sith *Zhawathk* (Acolytes) will need to learn Borgal and visit the Black Temple. Below are some introductory words and concepts. More information will be made available to students of *Chuzwan* (Apprentice) rank or higher, and in future books from Sith Academy.

Vowel Pronunciations:

û ("hoot")

u ("hut")

â ("hat")

a ("hot")

i ("hit")

î ("heat")

ai ("high")

o ("hole")

Pronouns:

I	*nam*
you	*chod*
he	*gun*
she	*gon*
we	*nûk*
they	*gram*
it	*ram*

Possessive pronouns are formed by prefixing "u" ("of") at the beginning:

unam my

uchod your

ugun his

ugon   her

unûk   our

ugram   their

uram   its

Possessive pronouns go after the noun they refer to. For example:

akâd unam   my book ("book of I")

vazûl unûk   our passion ("passion of we")

Nouns:

akâd	book
Borgash	Dark Lord
châzut	sorcery
chozâk	planet
dâg	cabal, cell
dûm	network
dwan	space, room
garath	master
gash	lord
gaz	brother, priest
gazûl	brotherhood
karzâth	empire
klan	chaos

raka, rak	power
rakadûm	imperium ("power network")
rakadwan	power space, dojo
shaka	glory
shaz	war
targ	year
thraz	fear
thûl	world
vazûl	passion
vril	the Force
zakshod	temple
zarg	fire
zhin	will
Zith	Sith
zûm	sun

Adjectives:

bor	black, dark
bran	weak
mal	white, light
vo	high, great
vra	all
zak	holy
zan	strong

Prepositions:

ag   in

am   to

raz   with

thra   from

u   of

vû   for

Verbs:

arkan   command

ash   is

dazh   hail

farg   write

gath   live

korz   know

kazh   liberate

maz   die

morz   struggle, train

mûkaz win, triumph

shuk   learn

thorak conquer

vadrat rise

vash   crave

zhot   go

Conjunctions:

iv   or

oz   and

Demonstratives:

chak   that

chad   this

chakz   those

chadz   these

Tense:

-al future (morzal = will train)

-ol past (morzol = trained)

-ûn present participle (morzûn = training)

Suffixes:

âg   to make (branâg = weaken)

ath   -er (vashath = craver)

bran   -less (rakbran = powerless)

shad   -est (voshad = greatest)

ûk   -ness (borûk = darkness)

ûl   -hood (borgazûl = brotherhood)

um   -en (fargum = written)

zan   -ful (rakzan = powerful)

zat   -ion (mûkazat = triumph)

zon   stay, continue (rakzanzon = stay powerful)

zoth   very (zanzoth = very strong)

Sample Sentences:

Nam ash ag rakadwan unam.   I am in my power space.

Gun morzûn vû shaz.   He is training for war.

Gram zhot am zakshod.   They go to the temple.

Nûk ash châzutathk u Zithgazûl.   We are sorcerers of the Sith Brotherhood.

Gon ashol rakzan.   She was powerful.

Chod ash vrilbran.   You are Forceless.

Vril kazhal nûk.   The Force will free us.

Common Sayings:

Thûl ash unûk!   The world is ours!

Nyaz morzûk!   Much struggle!

Rak am chod.   Power to you.

Borzon.   Stay dark.

Dazh am Karzâth oz vada gath Zith!

    Hail to the Empire and long live the Sith!

Vra rak am Zith!   All power to the Sith!

Power Symbols

"SIGNS AND SYMBOLS RULE THE WORLD, NOT WORDS NOR LAWS." -CONFUCIUS

The Dark Lords believe strongly in the power of symbols, to reorder the mind, focus the will, and awaken passions in the HUZNARG (mind-shadow) of dark side disciples.

Growing up in modern civilization, you have been bombarded by symbols from birth. They may take the form of corporate logos, government flags, sports emblems, religious icons, political posters, musicians' logos, etc. Such symbols are used to reinforce the cultural programming of the dominant orders of sorcerers – to invade and program your mind so that it will conform to their various agendas.

As Sith, we must deprogram and reprogram our minds from such conditioning, so that we may liberate ourselves from light side mental slavery and awaken our inner reserves of dark side power. This is a two step process. First, we mentally quarantine ourselves from the programming of the light side orders, by simply removing their symbols from our sight, or by developing enough awareness to be able to mentally nullify their effects at will. Second, we create new symbols of power which we have summoned from the huznarg, and begin consciously reprogramming ourselves with them.

This symbolic reprogramming process can take many

forms; you may put your power symbols on clothing, flags, walls, books, web pages, videos, or anywhere else your attention may turn. Remember that the real power of symbols is their ability to bypass the conscious mind, which contains filters that resist their influence, and work directly upon the subconscious mind, which is the source of our greatest power as Sith.

Below are a few power symbols the Dark Lords have created for this purpose. In the early stages of your training, Acolytes should adopt these to reinforce the message that you are part of an Order of Dark Lords, and you are submitting to their superior knowledge and power. But as you progress on your path, you should begin to develop your own symbols, and use them to establish your unique persona as an aspiring Dark Lord and master of symbolic sorcery.

Print out one or more these power symbols and place them in your power spaces. Click the images for full-size versions.

Nonagram

The nine-pointed symbol of our order is called the Sith Nonagram, or *Grazbrûg* ("nine-star") in the Black Tongue. Its nine points represent the Nine Echelons of Sith mastery which all Acolytes must complete to become Dark Lords. They also represent the Nine Pillars, Nine Maxims and Nine Canons which are the foundation of our ideology. The three red points symbolize the Three Paths (Zwo-Zovratz) of Matter, Transcendence and Self-Deification, with the latter Path reigning supreme over the other two at the top of the Nonagram. The points of the Nonagram also represent the Nine Mental Weapons of the Sith Master: will to power, willpower, formlessness, fearlessness, intelligence, imagination, persuasion, perception, endarkenment.

Imperial Sun

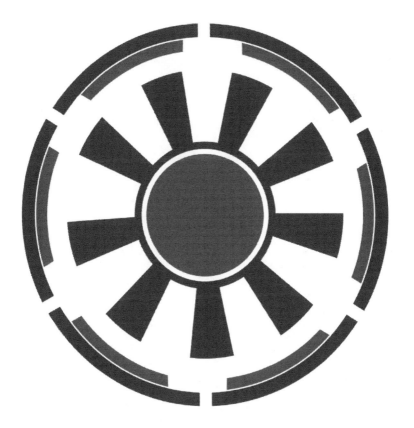

The Imperial Sun symbol is the emblem of our new Empire, to be worn by all soldiers and officials of the Sith Imperium. Its nine black rays symbolize the rising sun of Sith power over this planet and beyond.

War Trigammadion

The War Trigammadion of Darth Siluzon (General of the Conquest of the Sith as foreseen by Darth Ravenus) is a symbol of the Sith wars of conquest and the triumph of the dark side yet to come.

Black Dragon

The Black Dragon is the symbol of the Force fire that Sith training ignites in our Acolytes, burning away all that is weak and passionless. It is also the name of our shadow army, which guards the Temples and expands the Empire. All hail the Black Dragon!

Black Sun

The Black Sun is our symbol of the metaphysical source of the dark energy or *vril* that surrounds us, penetrates us and drives the galaxies apart. Wherever he may find himself in this vast universe, the endarkened Sith Lord should always be attuned to the Black Sun's rays, and draw upon their power just as a plant feeds upon the energy of the white sun.

Every Sith is like a star, moving on its own path around the galaxy. Just as stars orbit around the center of the supermassive black hole at the heart of every galaxy, so every Sith disciple's path is governed by the metaphysical gravity of the Black Sun. The unity of the physical black hole and the metaphysical Black Sun is one of the mysteries of our faith – pay respect to it by facing the Galactic Center during important meditations and rituals. From earth, the Galactic Center is located behind the "Dark Rift" of dust clouds in the Milky Way, near the Sagittarius constellation. Like the Kabaa stone of Islam, this should serve as your spiritual center wherever you may find yourself in this vast, dark universe.

The Black Sun is also our symbol of the Age of Endarkenment that is about to befall this planet. For the Dark Lords have foreseen that an eclipse is near for the light side order, and the Dark Side will soon prevail. Watch the sky with your third eye: the rise of the Black Sun heralds the victory of the Sith!

Skull Sign

The Skull Sign (KRUKOZÛM) is a symbol used to communicate with Darth Omega by Dark Lords Ravenus and Imperius, using symbolic sorcery such as the Skull Stare. The Omega Transmission tells of a time when the suns went black and doom came to his galaxy, as foretold by an ancient Sith prophecy. The Dark Lords believe this is a warning to all who dare stare into this Pandora's Box of Death that our stars, too, will go black, and our universe will die.

Death's Head

The skull-and-crosshairs or death's head (MAZÛKRUK) symbol may be used by Sith Assassins to mark anything targeted for death by the Empire.

Banners & Flags

This is the Sith imperial flag, for use in Temples, Rakadwans, gatherings, and ultimately to be flown over all this planet's power centers.

This banner symbolizes the founding of the Sith Temple -- the first dark side temple in this galaxy -- and the rising of the sun of Sith power over this planet.

The Sith imperial flag waving above planet Earth and against the background of the Milky Way galaxy symbolizes the victory of the Sith and the foundation of our Galactic Empire.

Sith Specializations

Sith Lords can come from any walk of life, and pursue any worldly career they desire. The essence of Sith mastery is to make the most of your potential and to acquire power in the way that is best suited to your abilities.

However, the Dark Lords have identified a number of specialized paths that are of particular interest to the Empire. These are paths that can benefit you in your mundane life, while playing important roles in the imperial power structure.

Below are the specializations we encourage you to choose from at Sith Academy. In future Echelons, your training may be specialized to reflect your choice, including a final series of trials in that field.

Sorcerer

Sith sorcery is the art and science of manifesting the Will, using symbols, language, rituals, myths, memes, technologies and other techniques of mental influence. A Sith sorcerer studies dark arts such as memetic engineering, worldview warfare, thought-bombing, mind tricks, hypnosis, drugs and power rituals, in an effort to acquire what all Sith seek: *unlimited power*. A Sith sorcerer is somewhat similar to a Sith Templar, but is less focused on philosophy and mysticism than in getting immediate results.

Assassin

The Sith assassin learns the methods of the shadow warrior: targeted killing, covert operations, extortion, espionage, sabotage and dirty tricks. Skills of the assassin include proficiency with handguns, rifles, blades, poisons and explosives, expertise in security, intelligence gathering, operational planning, tracking, stealth, evasion, deception and survival. The Sith assassin learns to survive in the shadows in all environments on this planet, and to track down and sanction anyone the Empire wants punished.

Industrialist

The Sith industrialist specializes in the creation or extraction of wealth. He may become a corporate executive, businessman, entrepreneur, investor, banker, trader or mercenary. He will focus on those industries that confer the greatest opportunities for wealth and power. In the present age, this means he is likely to be a technology entrepreneur, venture capitalist, arms manufacturer or resource baron. He studies the principles of business administration, leadership, entrepreneurship, finance, social manipulation and personal influence.

In this era, money rules the world. Therefore, the Dark Lords strongly encourage our students to pursue careers in business and industry, so they will be well placed to accumulate wealth and power for the Empire.

Politician

Politicians are an unfortunate necessity in today's world. Despite the increasingly oligarchical nature of most political systems, there is still considerable power to be gained through the conventional political process. While democratic systems are by their nature abhorrent to Sith Lords, we are more than willing to play the game and manipulate, infiltrate and subvert them to our ends. Therefore, we are always interested in recruiting and grooming individuals with strong political aptitude and connections, who will eventually be called upon to use their positions of influence to further the power of the Empire.

Scientist

The Sith scientist studies the properties of the material world, in order to understand and exploit them for the benefit of himself and the Empire. Areas of particular interest to the Empire are fields such as longevity research, transhumanism, cyberwar, artificial intelligence, parapsychology, space propulsion, weapons research and nuclear physics. Such fields promise to greatly increase the power of the human species, and the Sith in particular. We therefore encourage anyone with the aptitude and interest to pursue a career as a Sith scientist.

Templar

The Sith Templar studies the philosophy, ideology and mysticism of the dark side religion. He seeks to understand and harness the mysterious power of the Force, operates Sith Temples, masters the rituals and liturgies of our Black Brotherhood, and learns to speak *Borgal* – the Black Tongue of the dark side. The Templar wages spiritual warfare against all competing priesthoods, while working to convert others to the dark religion using every method of personal influence, mystical working and social manipulation.

Commander

The Sith commander is a master of the arts of war. He studies military strategy, tactics, intelligence, logistics, training, technology and leadership. He may be a high-ranking officer, elite soldier or a civilian defense expert in any nation in the world. He will seek the highest ranks in the most powerful branches of the military, according to his aptitude and society. He might become a general, a special operations commander, a defense chief, high-ranking advisor or intelligence executive. When the time comes for the Sith to seize power, commanders may be called upon to provide information, material or operational support for a coup, revolution or all-out war of conquest.

PRAXIS

Sith Training: Daily Practices

To develop the powers of a Sith Lord, one must first develop a basic understanding and mastery over the Dark Side of the Force. This is not an *easy* process, but those acolytes who pursue this path find that they make progress much *quicker* than those who follow the Light-side paths.

Power is our passion,
War is our Way,
Darkness is our Destiny
The Force will set us free.

True Power begins with a genuine craving for power. There is a Sith saying: *Vra rak am Zith* ("all power to the Sith"). So then, what is power? Power (*raka*) is control over oneself and one's environment. The true Sith are distinguished by their personal, regional, and social control. To develop this control, the Sith develops powers of mind and body, in order to impose and maintain their personal power over their environment.

Through power, through victory, the Sith attain freedom, which means the ability to live according to their own desires and wisdom, and not to be ruled by others.

In order to develop *power*, the Sith must develop first the Will (*zhin*) necessary to wield the Force. While indeed the Force (*vril*) flows through all beings, very few are able to tap into this innate power, and none can do so without a powerful Will.

The aspiring acolyte will make use of the following daily practices. Acolytes should feel free to innovate and add their own disciplines, but should consult with their master beforehand.

Sith Training: Physical Trials

The Sith are constantly testing themselves, striving to rise above their current state at all times. The Dark Side is not a path of pure contemplation – rather it is a path of passion and activity. Just as one tempers a blade of steel through immersion in fire, the Sith seeks to test and refine the body through trials. So as part of their daily routine, all Sith acolytes must engage in a program of physical fitness. This can involve cardio-vascular training (climbing, running, swimming), strength training, yoga, or martial arts. Cross-training is especially good, though more challenging.

As part of your Sith training, select a physical training routine that is possible to pursue on a daily basis. This means examining your environment and perhaps having to locate a gym or dojo. It may be necessary to try several types of sports or fitness routine in order to find one to which you will respond well. Securing a trainer or teacher is ideal, though virtual trainers are available on the internet for those whose circumstances do not allow access to live sessions.

TRIALS

In coordination with your fitness trainer (or Sith master), devise physical trials to be enacted each three months. The trials should be a step above your regular routine, and each trial should be harder than the one previous to it. Failure is not an option, and is an indication that you are not taking the training seriously.

Record the trial in your Sith journal, and share the results in the form of a progress report with the Sith masters at **sithacademy66@gmail.com.**

Sith Meditation: Diamond Body

The teachings of the Sith demand that an acolyte develops a powerful mind and will, which can in turn only be housed inside a powerful body. To neglect the body is dangerous, for the acolyte who does so learns that the Will burns inside as a flame, and consumes the flesh if the body is not properly trained. The Dark Side especially is dangerous, as it opens the acolyte to contact with powerful and volatile Force energies and clementals, and so the flesh must be hardened like steel in order to properly harness them. The Sith practice of Diamond Body meditation allows the Sith to use the

Will to harden the body, protecting themselves from internal energies and also from external threats. **NB.** *Believe that this is not merely a visualization, but a willed evolution on the physical level.*

PRACTICE

Begin the meditation in your *rakadwan* (temple). Assume a seated position, cross legged on the ground. Maintain a relaxed, upright position. Slow your breathing, so that you feel a sense of calm detachment.

A. Visualize yourself in detail, as you are currently, from your head to your feet. Become aware of your strengths and weaknesses on a physical level.
B. Now visualize an evolved Sith version of yourself. This form has no weaknesses. It is hard and strong, like a black diamond. It regenerates from harm quickly, and does not easily age or become tired or sick.
C. Focus on becoming this new being. See your body changing, shifting into an idealized, supernatural version of yourself. You are still you – human – but now harder and sharper, like a black diamond. The Force flows freely through your veins now, changing you, making you stronger and stronger with each moment.
D. Maintain this core meditation for at least 30 minutes. Repeat during the day when you feel tired or weak.

POST-PRACTICE

- As you embrace this practice, the Force will direct you to various opportunities to create the new body. You may feel the urge to begin a particular sport or exercise regime.
- Your appetites and eating habits may change drastically, as the new body begins to impose itself on you. Embrace those opportunities and urges.
- Maintain a daily written record of your experiences. At the end of the month, write an evaluation of the change in yourself and in your behavior. Be critical and direct. After one month, submit the evaluation to **sithacademy66@gmail.com**.

Sith Meditation: Force Body

The teachings of the Sith demand that an acolyte develops a powerful spirit, in order to sense the Force and to direct it towards the goals of the individual Sith and also those of the Sith Empire. To do so requires the conviction that the Sith themselves are both physically and psychically evolved creatures. Most humans operate primarily in the physical world, and so they have a good sense of their physical plane. However the Sith operate also on the Force plane, and so they must develop a sense of the Force Body. The Force Body is that part of the Sith which is used in dreams and in trance states, and allows the Sith to take part as an active player, instead of as a spectator or helpless victim like most other humans. The Sith practice of Force Body meditation allows the Sith to use the Will to generate their own Force Body, which is a key practice to more advanced Sith techniques.

PRACTICE

Begin the meditation in your *rakadwan* (temple). Assume a seated position, cross legged on the ground. Maintain a relaxed, upright position.

A. Visualize yourself in detail, as you are currently, from your head to your feet. Be aware of yourself as a spiritual being, in whatever state you normally choose to do so, such as a soul, ghostly presence, glowing light, aura, etc.

B. Now visualize a powerful Force being. It is useful to picture a famous Sith Lord or elemental spirit or antihero (or similar image). Pay attention to details as much as you can, such as spiritual armor, weapons, accoutrements, etc. Take note of the colors, the textures, the sensations of this new shape.

C. See your spirit condensing into this new powerful Force Body. Feel the Force flow through you, infusing this new body with raw power. Feel the passion within you taking actual shape on the spiritual plane, manifesting in your Force Body.

D. See your Force Body radiating a seething red nimbus of energy. This is the Force itself, which covers and protects your Force Body from harm.

E. Maintain the Force Body for at least 30 minutes.

F. When you have completed your time in the spiritual plane, imagine the Force Body re-integrating into your physical body. It is within you, and will empower you throughout the day.

POST-PRACTICE

- As you embrace this practice, it is possible that you will become increasingly aware of the Force energies in your local environment. These can be channeled more effectively, once you are aware of them.

- If there are Force spirits nearby when you practice this meditation, it is very likely that their presence will become evident. Do not be alarmed or distracted, but make note of strange "happenings" that result from this particular meditation.

- Maintain a daily written record of your experiences. At the end of the month, write an evaluation of the change in yourself and in your behavior. Be critical and direct. After one month, submit the evaluation to **sithacademy66@gmail.com**.

Sith Meditation: Dark Mantras

The Sith hold that the Will can be better directed when certain tools are used to focus it. One of the most effective tools is that of the spoken word, sometimes called *mantras* by Light-side traditions, otherwise called *brazutk* by the Sith. Through a combination of meditation, speech, and the Will, the Sith is able to create powerful internal changes within themselves, and external changes in the rakadwan (temple) and the environment. Mantras reprogram the minds of acolytes so that they work in unity with the Force currents of the Sith empire. Further, real mantras also serve to change the very nature of the Force in the region where they are practiced. A potent mantra will have a cascading power effect, where it creates change in the acolyte,

SITH ACADEMY: THE PATH OF POWER

then the *rakadwan*, then the localized area surrounding the *rakadwan*. Mantras should not be invented by the acolyte, and most must be transmitted from master to apprentice. However, the Sith Academy encourages all potential acolytes to practice the following mantra exercise, in order to awaken their Sith potential. Genuine mantras of the Sith Academy are always in the Borgal language. **NB.** *The use of mantras can be dangerous, if approached haphazardly or without proper guidance. Use only in consultation with a master.*

PRACTICE

Begin the meditation in your *rakadwan* (temple). Assume a seated position, cross legged on the ground. Maintain a relaxed, upright position.   Slow   your breathing, so that you feel a sense of calm detachment.

A. Clear your mind of all distractions, so that your consciousness is centered on the Force.   Feel it flowing through you and around you.   There is nothing except the Force.
B. After 5 minutes of meditation on the Force, begin to recite the following mantra aloud on the exhaled breath, and silently on the inhaled breath.

  ▪ *NAM ASH ZAN AG ZHIN (I am strong in Will).*

C. Continue recitation for at least 15 minutes.
D. As you chant, focus on the sounds of the mantra. Feel it vibrate within you and around you. Visualize its vibrations causing the Force to gather within you and strengthen you.

E. Be aware of the change within your own Force energies. Be mindful also of the way that the Force changes within the confines of the *Rakadwan*.

F. Conclude the session with 5 minutes of silent repetition of the mantra. During this time, repeat the mantra on the inhalation and exhalation, but internally and silently.

POST-PRACTICE

- As you embrace this practice, you will feel the Force much more keenly than in the months prior to the practice. You will also find that concentration and meditation becomes easier with each passing week of practice.

- Throughout the day, when you wish to empower yourself through the Force, repeat the mantra silently for several minutes.

- Maintain a daily written record of your experiences. At the end of the month, write an evaluation of the change in yourself and in your behavior. Be critical and direct. After one month, submit the evaluation to sithacademy66@gmail.com.

Echelon One Challenges

Introduction

The first Echelon of Sith Academy training is about demonstrating your craving for power and establishing your Sith persona – it's your first step into the larger, darker world of the Sith Lords.

When you think about the great Sith Lords of legend, what comes to mind? Surely it is their awesome presence, their intense lust for power, their unbreakable will and their powerful individuality, among other things. Is this not the kind of power, passion and individuality you crave for yourself?

Don't believe the light side lie that the Sith Lords are "villains" and "bad guys"! In reality, they are powerful models for the kinds of beings each of us longs to be, deep within our souls. The purpose of this Echelon is to explore your "inner Sith Lord" and begin developing your individual, exceptional Sith persona.

To complete Echelon One, study the nine lessons below and take the actions described. Questions about this material can be emailed to **sithacademy66@gmail.com**.

Hail to the Empire and long live the Sith!

Challenge 1: Your Space of Power

You should establish a space of power (*Rakadwan* in our dark tongue) for your Sith meditations, rituals and exercises. This could be a room or part of a room where you keep your meditation and exercise equipment, weapons (sword, knife, lightsaber, staff, etc.), masks, banners and other items used in your training. It could also be a location outdoors where you feel the Force strongly. Be sure to include at least one weapon in your Rakadwan — a Sith should never be caught unarmed!

We encourage you to put a Nonagram or other power

symbol in your Rakadwan to show your allegiance to our Sith vision. Our power symbols are explained later in this book and can be printed out at **sithacademy.com/power-symbols**.

Once you have set up your Rakadwan, take at least one picture and/or video and email it to **sithacademy66@gmail.com** or contact us by Skype: sithacademy.

Challenge 2: Your Vision of Dark Lordship

Write a short story or make a video describing a vision of yourself as a Dark Lord of the Sith. Describe your appearance, temple, training, conquests, etc. Give us a detailed idea of how you imagine the Sith Empire will manifest itself on this planet, and your role in it. Your story should be at least 2-3 pages long, double-spaced. Email your story or video to **sithacademy66@gmail.com** or contact us by Skype: sithacademy.

Challenge 3: Your Uniform

Another thing you should do to commit yourself to the Sith Path is acquire an Acolyte uniform. A good choice is a black ninja, kendo or karate uniform, which also makes an excellent underlayer to wear beneath your Sith robe (which will be provided to you later in your training). You can also create your own Acolyte uniform using whatever clothing you have or can make, such as a hoodie, black t-shirt, comfortable pants and half-mask.

It's important to understand that this uniform is not a form of cosplaying or LARPing. Like martial arts organizations, priesthoods and the military, when you begin to wear your uniform during your practice, it will change the way you think and get you to begin living in your new, more powerful Sith persona.

When you have your Acolyte uniform, take pictures or videos of yourself wearing it, preferably with a weapon and a powerful Sith pose. Email the images/video to **sithacademy66@gmail.com** or contact us by Skype: sithacademy.

Challenge 4: Creating a Mask

"All great things must first wear terrifying and monstrous masks in order to inscribe themselves on the hearts of humanity."

As Sith, we create masks for many reasons. We create them to disguise our true nature and identity. We create them to awe and terrify our enemies. We create them to shock ourselves out of our conditioned personality and take on a dark new persona. We create them because it sometimes takes a mask to face the dark truth.

Your first task is to create a mask that you can use to construct your Sith warrior persona and disguise your face in visual communications with other Sith. The mask can be made from scratch using whatever materials you like, or you can purchase an existing mask. Be sure the mask covers the area around your eyes. Use the Force to call up a powerful mask from the dark side of your mind.

Here is a picture of a mask being created from scratch by a Sith Academy Acolyte:

Here is an example of a mask that was purchased and modified by one of our Acolytes:

Always remember that as Sith, we are to remain secretive and should never reveal our real selves to others, including our fellow Sith Academy students. We are formless, adaptable, and can create whatever mask is necessary to acquire power.

Once you have created your mask, you will need to take a picture or video to document that you have done so. You may email us an image or video to **sithacademy66@gmail.com** or contact us by Skype: sithacademy.

Challenge 5: Saber Salute & Mantra

This exercise will begin to develop your *Rakvashûk* (power-craving) using the power of the lightsaber, sound and ritual. It also develops control of your mind and body in preparation for Echelon Two: Willpower.

You should have a high quality lightsaber for this Challenge. You may use a sword, staff or similar weapon for now, but you will need to acquire a good lightsaber later in your training.

Go to your Rakadwan and put on your uniform and mask. Stand up straight with your arms to your sides, the lightsaber in your right hand. Quickly bring your saber hand to your chest, then punch it straight out and hold the saber in a vertical position. Your arm should be angled slightly upward. This is the "Saber Salute" or "Sith Salute".

In the Saber Salute position, begin chanting the Sith

Academy Mantra, preferably in our Black Tongue:

Rak ash vazûl unûk.
Shaz ash vodûn unûk.
Borûk ashal twazûl.
Vril kazhal Borgazûl.

[Translation:]

Power is our passion
War is our way
Darkness is our destiny
The Force shall set us free

Chant in a steady, powerful rhythm, and focus your gaze on the saber blade. Keep your body still, the saber vertical and don't let your arm drop. Do this for at least 5 to 10 minutes. To finish, bring your saber hand back sharply to your chest, then down to your side. Email a video of yourself doing this exercise to **sithacademy66@gmail.com** or contact us by Skype: sithacademy.

Note: You may also try staring at one of our power symbols while you do this mantra to focus your attention and increase your Force power. Power symbols are described later in this book and can be printed out at **sithacademy.com/power-symbols**.

Also, start thinking about a unique power symbol that represents your Force power. Every Acolyte will need to create such a symbol to become a Dark Lord.

Challenge 6: Evaluating Your Sith Persona

Read "The Exceptional Sith Persona," located in the "Ideology" section of this book. Now answer the following questions, either in writing or by video (the preferred method of communication with us).

1. Describe some of your greatest hatreds in life – it could be a person, an idea, an experience or something else. How do these hatreds motivate you? How do you repress or act on these hatreds now, and how would you like to act on them in the future?
2. Whom or what do you currently serve? Do you serve them willingly, or unwillingly? Why?
3. Read the "Sith Specializations" section of this book and choose the specialization that most interests you. Which specialization did you choose and why? Be detailed.
4. Describe your "internal empire" – a vision of a different world that inspires and motivates you. What are you doing to manifest that world?
5. Who do you think are some of the most powerful "Jedi"/light side factions on this planet, and how can they be defeated?

Submit your written or video answers by email to **sithacademy66@gmail.com** or contact us by Skype: sithacademy.

Challenge 7: Power-Craving Sermon

The Nine Mental Weapons are nine ways the Sith Master uses his mind as a tool for acquiring power. In Echelon One, we require the Acolyte to demonstrate the first Mental Weapon: Power-Craving ("Rakvashûk" in our Dark Tongue).

Assignment:

Read "Maxim One" in the "Ideology" section of this book to get a better understanding of what is meant by Rakvashûk (pronounced "rock-VAW-shook"), and why it is so important to the Sith.

For this challenge, you should also acquire the Sith Imperial podium/altar cloth with the Sith nonagram symbol, which you can use in your sermons and personal rituals, or wear on your arm. The podium cloth is available at **templeofthesith.com/shop.**

When you are ready, put on your Acolyte uniform and go into your Power Space. Put the podium cloth in an appropriate place or wear it on your arm. Hold this book in your hands and imagine that you are delivering an inspirational sermon at your own Sith Temple. Search your feelings and awaken your Rakvashûk. Do you feel it? That's the power of the Dark Side!

Make a short video of yourself delivering this sermon, discussing and demonstrating what power-craving means to you. You may wish to read and discuss a passage from this book. When you are done, email the video to **sithacademy66@gmail.com** or contact us by Skype at handle "sithacademy".

Challenge 8: Protocols of the Sith Illuminati

Sith Lords are always devising protocols, plans and stratagems that will allow us to increase our power and expand our Empire. We study classic works of strategy like Sun-Tzu, Machiavelli, The Protocols of the Elders of Zion and the 48 Laws of Power, and record our strategy ideas in Sith Academy books and also private holocrons, for use by other Sith Apprentices and Lords.

For your next challenge, propose at least one Sith "Protocol" or "Law of Power" of your own. Write it up in detail — it should be at least 600 words — and email it to us at **sithacademy66@gmail.com**. You may wish to consult some of the classic strategy books listed in the **Sith   Academy Library** (http://sithacademy.com/publiclibrary/) for ideas.

THE PROTOCOLS OF THE
SITH ILLUMINATI

A GUIDE TO A NEW GALACTIC ORDER

Challenge 9: Acolyte Pledge

You have reached the final Challenge of Echelon One, and it is time to leave your computer and your Rakadwan and make a stronger connection with the Dark Lords of the Sith. We advise great discretion in this trial: let no one else know what you are about to do, for your own sake and the sake of the Empire.

This task is critical because it will allow us to exchange items and communicate via the mail system if our internet connection is somehow compromised. You should establish a way for us to contact you by mail other than providing your home address. This can be done by paying for a Post Office Box or simply registering a General Delivery address with your local post office, which can usually be set up for free. If neither of these options is available, you can use your home address, but this is strongly discouraged.

Once you have done this, hand write the following Acolyte Pledge in the Dark Tongue on a piece of paper:

Nam chom rabûk am Borgashk
U Zithgazûl ag chad brûkthuz
Oz am Rakadûm gam arkan
Vat Karzâth, nazg vril banthorzhinugrak
Raz mûkazat oz raka vû vraskâshk

Translation:

I pledge obedience to the Lords
Of the Sith Order in this galaxy

And to the Imperium which they command,
One Empire, in the Force indomitable,
With victory and power forever.

Sign the Pledge with your Sith name and signature or personal symbol.

Additionally, we would like a personal artifact from you that we can place at the main Sith Temple of the Dark Lords. This could be any item that has power to you, such as a token, weapon, article of clothing, etc. By sending us an artifact of power to be placed at our Temple, you will open a Force connection between us that can empower you across space and time. If you would like to make other contributions to the Order, send those also.

Your Acolyte Pledge, personal artifacts and offering should be mailed to the following address:

SA
PO Box 2621
Everett, WA 98213

Once we receive your items, we will determine if you are ready for Apprenticeship, or if other tasks are required to complete Echelon One. If chosen for Apprenticeship, you will be assigned to study at the **Temple of the Sith** to become a Sith Templar, or remain at the Academy as an Apprentice and prepare for a leadership position in the Sith Imperium.

Training Notes

Use this space for notes related to your Echelon One Training.

Praxis

EPILOGUE

This book has been a record of the key revelations, thoughts and works of the Dark Lords of Sith Academy since Imperial Year One. It is the ideological foundation of our Order, and a roadmap to future conquests. If the Dark Lords are ever killed and the Sith Order destroyed, this book should be enough to allow a *vrilzan* person to rebuild it. If you find yourself in such a time, perhaps it is your destiny to do so.

The Sith must always survive, and seek victory across time and space. With this book we are calling out to others to continue our great legacy. Recall the final words of Darth Omega to Darth Imperius:

"Remember, young prophet of your galaxy, that only the Dark Side can defeat death. Through you, the Sith will be reborn. Through you, the Sith will live forever. For in this dark universe, the Light is fleeting, but the Darkness is eternal."

If you have come this far and wish to continue your journey into the eternal Darkness, you will need to acquire book two of *The Nine Echelons of Sith Mastery* series. Until then, we bid you darkest farewell.

The Dark Lords of Sith Academy,

Imperial Year 4 (April, 2015)

Rak ash vazûl unûk

Shaz ash vodûn unûk

Borûk ashal twazûl

Vril kazhal Borgazûl

.

Nûk ash Borghashk u Zithgazûl.
Chad ash borzakshod unûk.

Doz ash Targ-u Rakadûm zwai
Nazg graz budrûmz u rak
Oz buldrokûn karzâthat drag
Nûk tharûz zakshaz unûk vragatûn

Nûk thorakal chad chozâk, chad brûkthuz, chad vrathûl
Kosh arkanol nazg Borgash Omega
Vratâgum nazg borvril
Drashum nazg Borzûm
Mûkazat ashal unûk!
Dazh am Karzâth oz vada gath Zith!

HAIL TO THE EMPIRE AND LONG THE LIVE THE
SITH!

12102644R10084

Printed in Great Britain
by Amazon.co.uk, Ltd.,
Marston Gate.